Central Heating

A design and installation manual

George Steele

Heinemann: London

William Heinemann Ltd
10 Upper Grosvenor Street, London W1X 9PA

LONDON   MELBOURNE   JOHANNESBURG   AUCKLAND

First published by Butterworth & Co. (Publishers) Ltd 1985
First published by William Heinemann Ltd 1986

British Library Cataloguing in Publication Data
Steele, George
    Central Heating: a design and installation manual
    1. Dwellings – heating and ventilation – amateurs' manual
    I. Title
    697'   TH7461

ISBN 0 434 91870 9

Photoset by Illustrated Arts Ltd., Sutton, Surrey
Printed and Bound in Great Britain by The Thetford Press Ltd., Thetford, Norfolk

Introduction

This book is a guide to modern domestic heating systems for those involved in the trade, for those studying the subject and for householders considering installing central heating. There is particular emphasis on avoiding the special problems that occur when the latest equipment is used.

I have been associated with the design and supply of central heating systems since 1966. Initially I wrote articles to convince inexperienced people that, with guidance, it was possible to install a perfectly sound heating system. Since then I have seen the growing confidence of ordinary people in their ability to tackle all types of jobs which would previously have been considered the sole province of professionals.

Now I am concerned at overconfidence; and not only by DIY people but also by the trade. Over the years more and more books and articles have appeared showing how easy it is to install heating, and any failures have generally been due to not bothering to find out how this or that piece of equipment is fitted.

The actual fitting of the parts is still as easy to learn as it always was; the calculations for heat losses, although now metric, are much the same and there is a wide range of information available. Then why, with so much more information now than years ago, are there more problems with radiator failures? Why, with all this extra central heating, do so many more homes suffer from condensation (which used to be associated with cold houses)?

The answer is that in the last five years advanced product design has brought about a revolution in system design. Not knowing this — and many professional installers are ignorant of the changes — causes considerable problems. At the same time, modern patterns of living coupled with a dramatic increase in the level of insulation have brought about damaging effects undreamed of in the early years of domestic heating.

In those days you knew that when you finished the installation and it worked, there was nothing more to worry about. Today, however, it is not enough just to fit the pieces together — you have to ensure that the system will not corrode away in a few years time; this entails learning a few new things such as positioning vent pipes and pumps differently from in the past.

Being involved commercially in the trade, I have become very aware of recent changes in attitude by manufacturers, particularly those who supply boilers and radiators. For many years, if a radiator or boiler failed in a short time, the manufacturers replaced it and often paid for incidental costs because, with the old system layout, failure was rare and was not worth arguing about. Now failure of equipment is such a problem, and the cause of it usually poor system design, that manufacturers are very selective about claims under guarantee.

It is no longer possible to blame the product if the fault is bad system design. The cost of replacing equipment will be borne by the installer, whether professional or DIY, and it could be costly. It is also apparent now that many steps taken to improve property by insulation cause expensive structural damage.

It is just as easy to do it right and avoid future replacement costs, and in this book I aim to make it as easy as possible for you to understand the reasons for the recent changes in design and why you can have a modern, safe and economic system with none of the problems becoming apparent in so many homes.

Because of these changes, I feel this is a good opportunity to look at heating from a new standpoint; not just as a means of heating the house but in conjunction with the house structure. We need to understand why heating systems and houses behave as they do rather than just go through the details of hanging radiators etc. (although this side is covered).

The manual skills required of a heating installer are not as difficult to master or as numerous as those of a plumber but there is a lot more to the theory. Don't rush into it; think about the kind of system suited to the home and the family needs. If you read it carefully, this book will enable you to have your 'afterthoughts' first and avoid being disappointed later. Always remember that the only true function of a modern heating system is the provision of human comfort.

The units used

I have used metric units throughout but anyone familiar only with the imperial system of measurement should have no difficulty in following everything. My aim is to make the subject understandable and to do this I may not follow standard SI metric notation.

The SI notation which the UK adopted is not the same metric system that has been in use on the continent for many years. People on the continent are only slightly less confused by SI than we are. The old imperial, and to a lesser extent the old continental centimetre-gram, systems were a patchwork of units which had evolved to serve the individual needs of different areas of scientific development in the 18th and 19th centuries. Each area was quite happy with its measurements but in more complex work, encompassing different areas, there was no system of measurement which could be used without tedious conversions. The SI has dealt with that problem but it has taken away the units and methods ideally suited to each individual area.

For example, some of the most serious problems in modern heating systems relate to differing water levels; these are caused by pressure variations which in SI units should be measured in pascals or newtons per square metre, and in the old centimetre-gram system in bars or millibars. In imperial for engineering the units would be pounds force per square inch. But for anything involving water the old measurement of pressure was in inches water gauge because pressure is proportional to the height of water above any point. In the metric system we can easily make a straight conversion to millimetres water gauge. This is better for the student of heating and water systems. It won't carry across as a useful means of measuring jet engine thrust but it is much more useful and descriptive in the single field of central heating.

For students familiar with SI units my explanations should give a different angle to things which will make a real understanding easier. For older readers brought up on the imperial method, while the units are basically metric, the principle of measurement suitable to the subject is retained. Because of this the book will also be useful as a bridge between the two systems. Remember, current students will have to work with people of greater practical experience but with a different way of looking at things.

In some areas strict SI units have been ousted by practical considerations. The imperial unit of energy is the British Thermal Unit (BThU); the SI unit is the joule. The imperial unit of power or heat transfer is the BThU per hour; the SI unit is the joule per second. When metrication was first adopted, recommendations were made by the metrication board concerning the units to be used. Many radiator manufacturers therefore started showing emissions in joules per second. Because the joule is a very small unit and because the watt was already used in the UK for electricity power ratings, very soon no-one was using the recommended units and now all radiator and boiler ratings are given in watts. So a strict adherence to recommended SI units will not help you select a boiler size without conversion.

Contents

1
Comfort

The first thing to consider is why we need heating systems at all. The reason is not to warm us up but to stop us losing too much heat. This may seem pedantic, but appreciating this point keeps our thinking in the right direction; we are looking for comfort, not a means of cooking ourselves.

Our body temperature is around 37°C while the highest acceptable room temperature is about 23°C. So we are always emitting heat to our surroundings just like a radiator or an electric fire.

Measuring heat

If you leave a cup of hot coffee it goes cold; if you put it in the snow it cools faster, so the rate at which heat is transferred is proportional to difference in temperature. The rate of transfer is measured in watts and, because the watt is a small unit, we often use a unit of 1000 watts called a kilowatt (kW).

Wherever the coffee is left, it will be colder after four minutes than after two. The total heat lost depends on the rate of loss and how long the rate is maintained. If an electric fire emits heat at a rate of 1 kilowatt for a period of 1 hour, it will transfer a total of 1 kilowatt-hour of energy (1 kWh). However, unlike the forgotten coffee, it does not get colder because the electricity generators provide replacement energy at the same rate as the fire is losing it.

Keeping warm

The average human rate of loss is 100 watts and in a party of 30 people the heat given out will be equivalent to a 3kW electric fire. Provided it is regularly stoked with food, the body can keep up with the loss just like electricity generators. It is only when the rate increases or decreases too much that we become uncomfortable and then we need some control over it.

The first controls were clothing followed by shelter even if only a cave dwelling. Up to the 19th century the dwelling was still the main protection. Fire was a bonus; the only fuel was wood, it was hard work getting it and, unless you owned the woods, quite expensive.

Homes were built for maximum protection at minimum cost, generally in sheltered spots with thick walls to store heat and low ceilings so that only a small volume of air had to be warmed. The windows were small and often omitted on the windward side of the house.

As fuel became cheaper houses were designed more for appearance and by the 1960s showed hardly any regard for conservation. Why bother? You could always fill up with cheap heat later. Things are different now. Fuel is again a luxury and we must return to the idea of the structure itself contributing more to our comfort.

Building heat losses

As mentioned earlier, when the body loses heat too rapidly we become uncomfortable. The obvious remedy is to keep our surroundings at a level acceptable temperature. However, when the house is heated, the temperature difference between it and the outside increases and it begins to lose heat itself. You can't just heat the rooms up to comfort level and then switch off; replacement heat must be provided continually at the same rate as the house is losing it. The heat is lost in two ways; by heat passing through the structure, and by warmed air being replaced with cold.

Heat losses through the structure

Different materials allow heat to pass through at different rates, indicated by U-values. The greater the surface area, and the lower the outside temperature, the greater the heat loss. The U-value therefore gives a rate of heat transmittance, in watts, for $1m^2$ of surface and for 1°C temperature difference between inside and out.

A rate of 3 watts per square metre for each degree difference would be written 3 W/m^2°C. I shall be dealing more comprehensively with U-values later but a few examples are shown in Table 1.1 together with the latest building regulations maximum permitted U-values. If your house has solid walls with a U-value of 2.13 W/m^2°C then they are losing over three times the heat of a new 0.6 W/m^2°C wall. The effect of changing regulations is shown diagrammatically in Fig. 1.1.

Table 1.1 Typical U-values

	U-value (W/m² °C)
Outside walls	
220 mm solid brick	2.13
Brick-cavity-brick	1.41
Brick-cavity-l/w block	0.95
Brick-foam-brick	0.56
Brick-foam-l/w block	0.47
Roofs	
Tiles on battens and felt plaster ceiling	2.08
As above with 50 mm insulation	0.60
As above with 100 mm insulation	0.34
Building Regulations maximum U-values	
External wall	
Wall between dwelling and ventilation space	
Wall between room and roof space	0.60
Floor between dwelling and outside air	
Floor between dwelling and ventilation space	
Roof including ceiling	0.35

Air-change losses

This loss is due to warmed air escaping through windows, doors etc. and fresh cold air entering. Each cubic metre of air needs 0.33 watt-hours of heat energy to raise its temperature by one

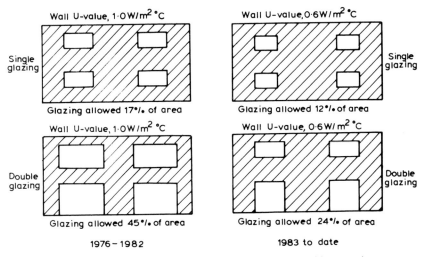

Fig. 1.1. The changing face of houses over the last few years. The 1976 Building Regulations appeared to be a drastic restriction compared with what had been allowed previously but they allowed some 'trade-off' in that the overall U-value of the perimeter could be 1.8 W/m² °C. So if the wall U-value were improved to 0.6 W/m² °C the area of window could be increased to around 25 per cent for single and 60 per cent for double glazing. Only seven years later the construction has been even more drastically curtailed and now there is no 'trade-off' permissible. What will the regulations be in 10 years time?

degree centigrade; this is the specific heat capacity of air. If the air is replaced every hour then a heating rate of 0.33 watts is needed for each degree rise.

If the air is changed twice in an hour then a rate of 0.66 watts is required. There are generally-accepted air changes to be used in calculations, and these appear in Chapter 12 for use in designing the system.

Outside design temperature

With both types of heat loss, the rate of loss depends on the difference between inside and outside temperatures. The inside temperatures are a matter of choice although there are recommended levels, which will be looked at in Chapter 12. However, in all countries there is a standard outside temperature used for heating calculation which represents average winter conditions. In the UK it is −1°C and I will use this throughout. Later on, under boiler sizing and running costs, I will put the case for lower outside temperatures.

We should not rush to provide heat to replace these losses without first considering whether they can be reduced by insulation and also what kind of heated environment will give us most comfort. For this it will help to know just how the body loses its heat.

Human heat losses

The various ways in which the human body loses heat are illustrated in Fig. 1.2. The first way in which heat is lost is by conduction. If you touch a window, it will feel cold; your warmth is conducted to the glass. We do not often place ourselves in a position where we are touching outer surfaces of a room and, although we are often in contact with other objects, the temperatures of these are not low enough to affect us, except in a room which has been unheated for a long time. Therefore, in relation to comfort we can ignore conduction.

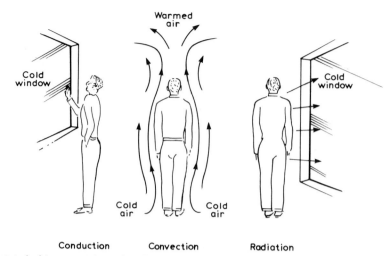

Conduction   Convection   Radiation

Fig. 1.2. Left: this person is losing heat by conduction to the cold glass, which is why it feels cold to the hand. Centre: this person is losing heat by convection and will be generally cooled all over. Right: heat is lost by radiation to the cold surface of the window and the cooling effect is felt only on the side nearest the window

The second way is by convection in which heat is first transferred to the air by conduction and then, because this air is warmer, it rises and is replaced by cool air which takes more heat away from the body. We lose a great deal of heat by convection which depends on air temperature and air movement. You feel colder in a draught even if the temperature is the same. This is the principle of the fan: it doesn't change the temperature of the air, it just moves it faster. However, air movement is not great enough in modern dwellings to take into account, and only the temperatures of the air is considered significant in convection loss.

Allied to convection is loss by evaporation, which also depends on air temperature and movement plus the moisture content of the air, known as its humidity level. Because humidity in this country is usually at an acceptable level for humans it is normally ignored in heating calculations but I shall come to it later in relation to condensation.

The last way is radiation, which does not need contact or air as a medium of transfer. This explains why you can feel quite warm in the sun's rays even when the air temperature is very low. So the two factors which have most effect on our comfort are the air temperature and the radiant temperature of surfaces surrounding us.

Surface temperatures

The temperatures of surfaces in a room vary more than air temperature and have considerable effect. A window may be as low as 5°C and a radiator as high as 75–80°C.

Of course, these different temperatures produce an overall average but the effect on the body depends on their relative positions. If there is a radiator at 75°C close to you on one side and a window of the same area at 5°C equidistant on the other, the average temperature of the two surfaces would be 40°C. This average is known as the mean radiant temperature (MRT) and in practice would also be influenced by all the other surface temperatures in the room, not just the window and radiator.

If you move closer to the window the radiator has less effect and the MRT at your new position may go down to, say, 20°C. Radiation loss from the body depends on the MRT at the position occupied, while convection loss depends on the air temperature.

Comfort temperatures

Although people vary in their comfort requirement, most feel comfortable if the average of air temperature and MRT is in the range 19°C to 23°C. If, for example, all surfaces were at 18°C for simplicity, as in Fig. 1.3, the MRT anywhere in the room will be 18°C. With an air temperature of 24°C, the average is 21°C. If you are comfortable at this combination, you would also be comfortable with the air at 20°C and MRT at 22°C because the average would also be 21°C.

This average, between MRT and air temperature, is used on the continent as a measure of comfort. It was devised by the Frenchman Missenard in the 1930s and is often shown in °M. The institutions concerned with heating in this country have recently adopted this as the scale for comfort but have called it the 'dry resultant temperature'; I find it easier and more descriptive to call it the 'comfort temperature'.

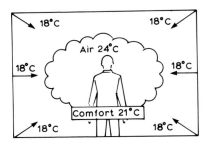

Fig. 1.3. In a room with all surfaces at 18°C and air at 24°C, the comfort temperature will be 21°C. In a normal room the surface temperatures vary and so the comfort temperature varies from one position to another

Inside comfort conditions depend on a combination of radiant and air temperatures, while those outside depend on the sun's radiation and air temperature. This outside combination is called the sol-air temperature. It is used in air-conditioning calculations but the solar effect is so small and unpredictable in winter that it is ignored in heating calculations and only the outside air temperature is used.

These comfort concepts explain many little-understood and often-argued points. It is not necessary to know about these in order to plan a simple heating system and install it; you could pass straight on to Chapter 12 for this, but I want to explain more than is usual so that you will

Table 1.2 Comfort temperature as percentage of air temperature

	Average U-value (W/m² °C)	No. of outside walls			
		1	2	3	4
Radiators	0.5	99%	98%	98%	97%
	1.0	98%	98%	96%	94%
	1.5	97%	96%	94%	91%
	2.0	96%	94%	91%	88%
	2.5	95%	92%	88%	84%
	3.0	94%	89%	85%	80%
Warm air convectors	0.5	96%	94%	93%	91%
	1.0	95%	92%	90%	87%
	1.5	93%	90%	87%	83%
	2.0	91%	87%	84%	80%
	2.5	89%	84%	81%	77%
	3.0	86%	81%	77%	73%

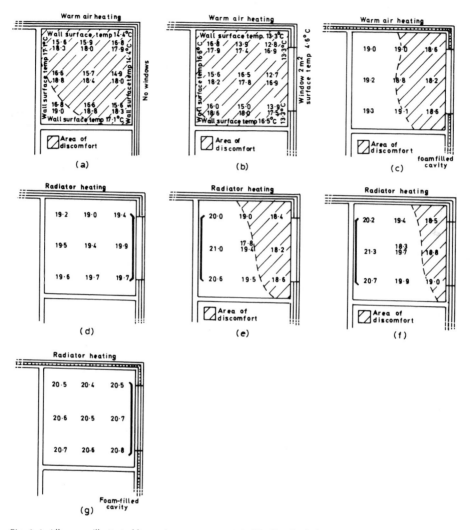

Fig. 1.4. All rooms illustrated have air temperature at 21°C. The shaded areas indicate discomfort below 19°C comfort.

Room (a) has brick cavity external walls (U-value 1.41 W/m² °C) and solid 220 mm internal walls (2.12 W/m² °C). There are no windors or doors and heating is by warm air or fan convectors. Average U-value 1.77 W/m°C. Room (b) is the same as (a) but has a 3m² window, which causes a larger area in which people will feel uncomfortable. Average U-value 2.07 W/m² °C. In room (c) the cavity has been insulated. However, the increase in wall surface temperature is not high enough to offset the cold window surface. Average U-value 1.73 W/m² °C. Room (d) returns to uninsulated cavity but the warm air heating has been replaced by a radiator under the window; the high surface temperature of this counters the window and there is nowhere in the room below the minimum of 19°C Comfort. Average U-value 2.07 W/m² °C. The radiator has been put on the inside wall of room (e) where it is not in a position to counter the window, and the area of discomfort is greater than in room (d). It has the same mid-point comfort temperature but in the rest of the room it is uneven. Average U-value 2.07 W/m² °C. Double glazing helps reduce discomfort zones but, as in (f), it does not even out the comfort level and an increase in air temperature would be necessary. Average U-value 1.86 W/m² °C. Room (g) is the ideal room with all the advantages; an insulated cavity, radiator under the window and double glazing. Average U-value 1.5 W/m² °C. The comfort temperature is 20.5°C at the centre of the room and is very even throughout. It is so close to the air temperature that the air thermostat is a reliable controller of our comfort at the outside design temperature. However it is still not exact, particularly at warmer outside temperatures

know your heating needs and the solutions better than most, and be better able to judge claims you might hear for this or that method, system or component.

If we want to be comfortable, we must achieve the comfort temperature we want. But we cannot measure comfort temperature; there are no thermometers readily available to record it. How can we find out what it is?

To make things simpler I have produced Table 1.2, which enables you to find approximate comfort temperature as a percentage of air temperature. Because the ceiling and floor effects tend to cancel out in any room in a normal house and to simplify things on the two-dimensional diagrams, I will ignore the small effect on MRT of these surfaces; the average U-value referred to is therefore that of all the walls, including windows.

In Fig. 1.4 various room conditions are illustrated; the comfort temperature is shown at nine different positions. In the first two I have also shown the MRT above each comfort temperature. The comfort temperature is the average of the MRT at each position, and the air temperature.

These comfort temperatures were worked out by computer using many factors but if you check the centre point in each room, you will find that the simplified table I have designed gives a close indication of the general comfort level represented by the comfort temperature at the centre of the room.

Where the comfort temperature is below 19°C the average person will feel too cold. To raise the comfort temperature it would be necessary to raise the air temperature, which uses more fuel.

You can see now why people are often fiddling with the room thermostat especially with a warm-air system. It is no good saying 'the system has been properly designed; leave the thermostat alone'. It may have been properly designed but on a day when the outside surfaces are cold, you need a higher air temperature to compensate and give comfort.

If the next day is very sunny, the outside walls warm up, the surface temperatures rise, and you turn down the thermostat because now you feel too warm. As you turn the thermostat down you glance at the thermometer and see that it shows exactly the same air temperature as the day before. Now you suspect the thermometer is faulty as well as the heating.

To improve matters we need to have surfaces which do not fluctuate so much with changes of outside temperature and to be able to use the air thermostat to control our comfort level with a minimum of correction.

To expect a thermostat to keep you comfortable without adjustment is asking too much. It is designed only to keep the air at a particular temperature; it cannot sense radiant heat as we can. Also a warm-air system heats only the air; it has little effect on the surface temperatures which affect us. Even with radiators much of the heat emitted is by convection.

Until someone designs a human 'comfortstat' the best thing is to create an environment where an acceptable comfort temperature can be achieved without a much higher air temperature so that the thermostat reading is more closely related to the comfort temperature.

You can now see that the type of heating you have, the position of radiators, double glazing and insulation all have an effect on surface temperatures and therefore on comfort levels.

2
The effects of heating

So far we have looked at heat losses with a steady indoor temperature, maintained by continuous heating, and an outside temperature of −1°C. If we turn the heating off for any length of time, obviously the air temperature will fall but so also will the temperature of the building itself. When the heating is switched on again it must not only provide heat for the steady-state losses but also raise the temperature of the structure.

Fortunately, when the inside temperature is low, the heat losses through the structure are lower because they are proportional to the difference in temperature. There is some spare heat therefore to raise the temperature of the structure but it is going to take some time.

The behaviour of buildings

The longer a structure has been unheated, the longer will it take to get up to temperature. The time taken and the energy required for reheating depends on the duration of the unheated periods and on the mass of the structure and its specific heat capacity.

I referred to specific heat capacity in connection with air-change losses. Generally, heavy dense materials have higher specific heat values, which means that they need more heat input to lift their temperature. Because of this the idea of 'weight' is often applied to buildings.

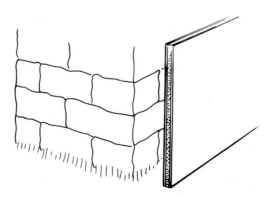

Fig. 2.1. The solid stone castle wall would be 2 m thick to equal the U-value of the 100 mm thick wall of wood and glass-fibre insulation. Here they are shown to scale. Of course, the thin wall has less structural strength, which is one of the problems with high-insulation value materials, but if it is no use for building castles and keeping attackers out it certainly keeps the heat in and would take only minutes to get up to temperature; the stone wall would take days

Continuous heating

If one building is constructed of lightweight materials such as timber walls with insulation between panels to give a Building Regulation U-value of 0.6 W/m²°C, and another is constructed of solid sandstone, the sandstone wall would be nearly 2 m thick for the same U-value.

It is often thought that it doesn't matter what materials are used as long as the U-value is the same. However, if the heating were to go off in, say, a hospital, it could be very serious and immediate steps would be taken to rectify the fault. While doing so, a lightweight building would cool so fast that soon the temperature inside could be close to that outside. A heavy stone building, on the other hand, would give out its stored heat over a longer period. It is obviously a good thing to create the required U-value of a continuously-heated building such as a hospital using heavy materials.

Intermittent heating

If a building is used only occasionally, say once a week, a massive stone structure would take so long to heat up that it might be necessary to switch the heating on three days before to get up to working temperature. A lightweight building which can warm up in an hour would be more suitable. You can see that the structure of a building should be related to its heating pattern.

You may think that this is not applicable to the domestic scene but there are many different materials now being used for housing, and the placing of insulation can also affect the 'weight' of a building, as will be explained in the next chapter on insulation.

Because of the extra heat required after each 'off' period, the running costs are not directly proportional to running time. If you heat your house for only eight hours per day and your neighbour heats his for 16 hours your bill will be more than half his; because of this it is sometimes recommended that it is more economical to run continuously. However, the economics depend on each individual case; on the pattern of use, the type of heating and the response of the particular house.

Response

Some way of measuring the extra heat necessary for warming up would be useful. However, energy flows are difficult to evaluate and only recently has the CIBS developed the concept of 'admittance' and 'Y-values' these are in the same units as U-values but represent the heat flow between the structure and the room in relation to changes in temperature. U-values represent energy transmitted through the structure and Y-values represent energy admitted into, or absorbed by, the structure itself.

A lightweight building will respond very quickly to heat input while a heavy building will respond slowly. If the admittance of heat into a wall (indicated by its Y-value) is the same as the transmittance (U-value) then the response ratio is 1 to 1. If the admittance is twice the transmittance, the response ratio is 2 to 1 and so on.

The response of the whole building depends on the proportions of different materials. For instance, windows absorb hardly any heat into the glass. When all the Y- and U-values for all the parts of a building have been evaluated and proportioned, we obtain the overall response ratio. There is no need for us to get involved with Y-values but I have mentioned them to explain how the responses in Table 2.1 are obtained.

If a 2.9 class of building were to be heated only once a week in winter, the heating system should provide about 2.9 times the heat output needed for steady-state heat loss in order to warm up the fabric reasonably fast. This is the kind of system sizing that is necessary with

Table 2.1 Response classification of structures

		Outer wall insulation		
	Nil	In cavity	On inside	On outside
Caravans		1.1	—	—
Recent houses (pitched roofs)				
335 mm brick-cavity-lightweight block				
75 mm lightweight block internal walls, solid floors	1.7	1.9	—	—
335 mm brick-cavity-brick				
105 mm brick internal walls, solid floors	2.0	2.4	—	—
220 mm solid-brick external walls				
105 mm brick internal walls, suspended wood floors	1.9	—	2.4	3.6
330 mm solid brick external walls				
230 mm brick internal walls, solid floors	2.5	—	2.6	3.9
Old houses (stone walls)				
460 mm solid external walls				
230 mm solid internal walls, solid floors	2.9			
640 mm solid external walls				
230 mm solid internal walls, solid floors	3.3			
Other buildings				
18th or 19th century church	from 4.0 to 5.0			
Medieval churches	from 6.0 to 7.0			
Castles, old cathedrals	from 7.0 to 9.0			

churches etc. However, with domestic property, even a slow-response one, the heating is on every day and little or no increase in size is necessary to allow for the warm-up period, although running costs are affected.

Domestic response

It might take only an hour to bring a house up to comfort level every morning. However, if you go away in winter and close the heating down for a week, on your return you will find that it takes a good bit longer than an hour; it might take over 24 hours with a slow-response property.

Most heating systems designed over the last 20 years are oversized. This is primarily because standard U-values were overstated until 1970, when more accurate measuring was possible. However, most calculations were made by rough rule of thumb or by using calculators, which for safety always over-sized. On top of this most installers went to a higher-rated radiator than necessary, again to be on the safe side. They then totalled the radiator emissions instead of the room heat losses and added an excessive 'cold weather margin' to determine the boiler size.

The resulting systems were quite often 50–70 per cent oversized; if since they were installed, the level of insulation has been improved, it is quite possible that systems are twice as large as necessary. Therefore the warming-up period is never a problem but it is by accident not by design.

Nowadays the cost of installation, even DIY, is considerable and no one wants to pay for a system twice as large as necessary. But if you calculate more accurately just the right heat losses it is more important to know about the response of the building if you are not going to get upset with a longer warm-up period than your friend whose heating was put in 15 years ago. He may have a rapid warm-up because his system is oversized but he is paying extra every day for its inefficient use of fuel.

System response

A building will take even longer to heat up if it has to wait a long time for the heating system to reach its operating temperature. As we saw in Chapter 1, greater comfort is created by incorporating some radiant heat. However, it takes some time for the water and the components to warm up and a quicker system response is obtained by warm air.

As with buildings, the more intermittent the heating the quicker the response required, but due to its lack of radiant heat, which necessitates a higher air temperature, many people do not like the warm-air atmosphere. In addition it is very difficult to fit into an existing house.

To get the best of both worlds we need a radiator system with as rapid a response as possible. This means reducing the water content and the mass of metal in the system because, like the structure, it all has to be heated up every time the system is switched on.

Apart from the use of specific components to reduce the water volume such as low-content boilers or microbore tube, response can be speeded up if the whole system is small in proportion to the property. This and many other advantages are provided by insulation.

3

Insulation

You will often see illustrations as in Fig. 3.1, giving percentage heat losses. This could be misleading because the percentages vary from house to house and they do not remain constant with increasing levels of insulation.

Table 3.1 shows losses totalling 15 000 watts from a typical house. You can see how the percentage loss from each component changes as different insulation is applied. The loss from the windows in the uninsulated house, in percentage terms, is 20 per cent, with the loft insulated it is 27 per cent, and with the walls insulated it is 23 per cent. But at all times the loss is the same at 3000 watts

Table 3.1 Heat-loss percentage variations

| | Uninsulated | | Roof insulated | | Walls insulated | |
	Watts	%	Watts	%	Watts	%
Cavity wall	3750	25	3750	34	1550	12
Windows	3000	20	3000	27	3000	23
Roof	4500	30	500	4	4500	35
Floor	1500	10	1500	14	1500	12
Air change	2250	15	2250	21	2250	18
Totals	15000	100	11000	100	12800	100

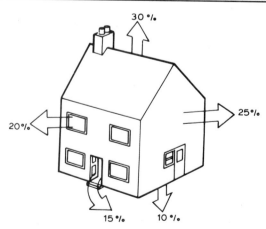

Fig. 3.1. A common but misleading way of stressing heat losses. With modern levels of insulation and different structures to conform with the new and very stringent building regulations, the percentages vary so much as to be meaningless

I do not intend to go into great detail about fitting the various products for insulation, which are always supplied with instructions anyway. I am more concerned with explaining the effect on comfort and costs. The important thing is to look at each method in cost-effective order and you will see an approximate pay-back time for each area in terms of fuel saving.

Draughtproofing

Draughtproofing is the first, cheapest and most obvious way of cutting down heat losses.

Doors

The gaps around doors can be dealt with in various ways as shown in Fig. 3.2, from a simple adhesive foam strip to long-lasting phosphor bronze strip. There are many types of draught excluder for the bottom of the door, and which one to use depends on the particular kind of door, sill and inside flooring.

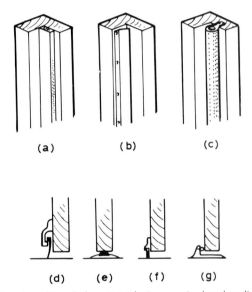

Fig. 3.2. Window and door draught excluders. At (a) the inexpensive but short-lived self-adhesive foam strip. At (b) a phosphor-bronze strip which will last at least 10 years; there is a plastic version which is much cheaper but which tends to become brittle with age. The neoprene seal at (c) is set into grooves machined into the frame; there are also neoprene self-adhesive strips. The door excluder at (d) is an automatic version, which lifts up as the door is opened. That at (e) is sometimes suitable but is more noticeable than the others. At (f), nylon bristles ride over the floor surface. The step excluder at (g) forms a seal when the door is closed on to it

Windows

The foam strip method can also be used with windows, but there are now some neoprene sealing strips which should last longer. If you are having windows made, you might consider having the frames machined to take specially shaped neoprene strips. A bonus is that when the window needs painting the strips can be removed, leaving a gap between the window and the frame, so that the windows can be closed while the paint is still wet.

Caution. Do not block up any air bricks. They were put there for a purpose and blocking them, especially if you have draughtproofed everywhere else, can cause problems.

Payback period for draughtproofing is from six months to one year.

Loft insulation

The next area in terms of value for money is the loft. There are many different materials available, the most popular being glass fibre, which comes in rolls. Over the years the recommended thickness has been 25mm, 50mm, 75mm and now 100mm; it will probably be 200mm in the near future (Fig. 3.3).

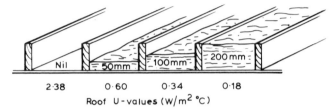

Fig. 3.3. Loft showing different U-values of complete roof (tiles on battens on felt and plasterboard ceiling) with varying thicknesses of insulation

Another method is to use Vermiculite granules; these are very light and can be spread between the joists. They are not quite as cost-effective as glass fibre and the depth is limited to the joist depth.

Pay-back period for glass fibre is two years and vermiculite is $3\frac{1}{2}$ years.

Cisterns and pipes

When applying loft insulation make sure that any cisterns in the loft are not insulated from the warm air below; ideally all cisterns and water pipes should be under the insulation not outside it. This is not easy in practice but failure to look to this point will cause more problems later; a burst pipe in the loft is not good news. All cisterns should have lids to reduce heat loss and condensation in the loft.

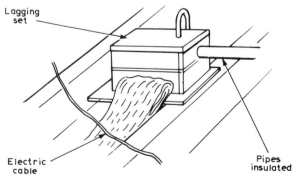

Fig. 3.4. When insulating the loft, take care to allow warmed air to reach the cisterns by not insulating under them. They themselves must be insulated around the sides and on top. Pipes must be insulated but electric cables must be kept cool

Electric cables

Unlike water pipes cables should be on top of the insulation. If insulation covers the cables, there is a possibility of overheating with the risk of fire — particularly when the wiring is old. If vermiculite is used, cables should not only be above but should not be in contact with it, since reaction may occur with the plastic covering.

Air supply

Insulation can cause problems the cost of which far outweigh any savings in fuel. The trouble is that the insulation keeps heat in rooms we use but makes other areas such as the loft much colder. In those areas moisture in the air condenses onto timber surfaces and both wet and dry rot can become established.

Regulations now require all structural timbers to be chemically vacuum-treated. However, that doesn't help those of us living in homes built before such treatments were available. What we can do is to make sure there is sufficient air-flow to take away the moisture before it condenses; this is dealt with in Chapter 4.

Wall insulation

Cavity fill

Cavity-wall insulation, particularly the U-foam type, has suffered more than any other insulation from scaremongering. There is no evidence that properly installed U-foam is any danger to anyone and, since it is the cheapest form of cavity insulation, this is important. However, it may not be suitable in exposed locations. An alternative is polystyrene pellets and another is blown mineral fibre.

In all cases, holes are drilled in the outer leaf of the wall and the insulating material inserted. The holes are quite small and the mortar is matched up afterwards so no marks can be seen. Obviously it is not a job for DIY people.

Pay-back time is three years for U-foam and four to five years for pellets and mineral fibre.

Solid walls

These are more difficult. The insulation can be put on the inside, which makes it necessary to refit window sills, skirting boards, electric cables etc. and can cause condensation problems. Insulation can be applied to the outside and covered by a special render, but this must be carried out by professionals.

Whether the insulation is outside or inside makes no difference to the U-value but it does make a difference to the response of the building. With the insulation on the outside the wall behaves like a heavy structure because the insulation slows down its loss to the outside. The wall is able to reach a higher temperature, which requires a greater energy input.

If the insulation is on the inside, the wall acts as a lightweight structure. The bricks never attain a high temperature so they need very little heat input. Because the bricks are on the outside, they cool down rapidly, giving up the small amount of heat they hold very quickly.

In Chapter 2 I pointed out the different response times needed for buildings according to their purpose. Of course no one these days is going to build a hospital of 2m stone walls to obtain a slow response but you can see how knowing where to place modern insulation can achieve similar results.

Pay-back time is seven to eight years for internal insulation and 20 to 30 years for external insulation.

Reflective panels

There are a number of reflective panels which are claimed to reduce the heat loss from radiators positioned on an outside wall. Some of the heat from a radiator is convected and some radiated. The wall is heated by these two components but, because of the closeness of the wall, the radiation component has most effect. It seems we have only to cut down the radiation into the wall to save some money.

A polished reflector certainly prevents heat getting into the wall. The trouble is that the heat doesn't go anywhere else; it stays in the radiator. The emission from the radiator is therefore less than its rated output. Because many radiators are oversized this reduction in output is not noticed but if your radiator has been accurately sized it might make a noticeable difference in cold weather.

After many experiments and calculations, I can say that a reflector panel saves approximately 2 per cent of the energy going through the wall but the radiator needs to be 12 per cent larger to give the same heat into the room than without the panel.

As a comparison, putting the radiator on an inside wall would save 4 per cent of the energy previously lost through the outside wall but comfort would be uneven as shown in Chapter 1. If the air temperature is increased to give acceptable comfort temperature throughout the room, the fuel costs will be the same as on an outside wall and the radiator would have to be increased by 4 per cent in size.

Floors

Heat lost through suspended wood floors can be reduced by filling in the cracks between the boards and covering with carpet and supporting insulation between the joists if there is enough space under the floor to gain access.

With solid floors most heat loss is around the edges. Some improvement is possible by putting a sub-floor of polystyrene covered with chipboard but it is hardly worth the trouble and expense if the edges aren't insulated, and you can't do that after construction.

Windows

More money is spent on double glazing than on any other form of insulation and yet it is the least cost-effective.

Secondary double glazing

With this method an extra window is fitted inside varying from quite simple fittings to elaborate plastic and aluminium channels in which properly edged panes of glass or perspex slide. As the air space between the panes is not sealed off, the effect on heat loss is not as good as a sealed unit.

Sealed units

The most common type has two sheets of glass with spacers to hold them the required distance apart. It is important that edges are hermetically sealed so that no moist air can get between the panes and cause condensation. The best insulation value is achieved with an air space of 20mm to 25mm.

Most sealed double glazing units are supplied complete with aluminium or UPVC frames but it is possible to have sealed units made to fit your existing wood frames at a considerable saving. If the rebate on the existing frame is not deep enough for the thicker double glazed units then special stepped units can be supplied (Fig. 3.5).

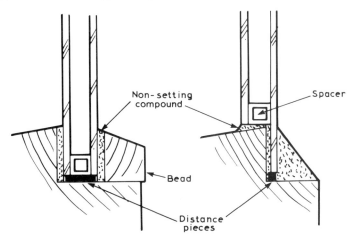

Non-setting compound

Spacer

Bead

Distance pieces

Fig. 3.5. On the left is a normal square-edge sealed unit fitted into a wood window frame. Where existing frames have rebates only deep enough for single glazing, special stepped units can be fitted as shown on the right

Pay-back period is five to seven years for secondary glazing and 20 to 30 years for sealed units depending on type.

Conclusions

Insulation is obviously necessary but careful thought is needed if it is to be economical, effective and safe. By that I mean a house where the pipes in the loft are not going to burst, where the electric cables are not being over-heated and becoming a fire risk and where the insulation is not encouraging rot because of excessive condensation, which is the No. 1 enemy of modern housing.

4

Heat and moisture transfer

Usually heat transmittance and U-values are thought of only in relation to building heat losses. However, with the ever-increasing risk of damage by condensation, the subject of heat transmittance should always be coupled with vapour transmittance, since this is at the heart of a proper understanding of domestic heating and its effect on buildings, condensation and people.

Thermal transmittance

If a wall is at the same temperature throughout and heat is applied to the inside surface, that surface will get hotter. The heat will start to conduct through the wall and if the wall is a poor conductor, i.e. has a high resistance to heat transmittance, it will conduct the heat away slowly; this gives the heated surface a chance to reach a higher temperature. So the higher the resistance, the greater the temperature difference between the heated side and the other.

This makes it possible to measure the thermal resistance of a structure by reference to the temperature difference between one side and the other, caused by applying heat at a rate of 1 watt to each square metre. The notation for this is $°C\ m^2/W$. If you look at the notation for U-values, in Chapter 1, you will see that it is $W/m^2°C$, which is the resistance notation reversed. This is logical and indicates that U-values measure the heat transmittance of a structure, which is the reverse of its resistance.

High resistance means low transmittance; when one is multiplied by the other, the result is always unity (1). A material with a resistance (R) of $0.25°Cm^2/W$ has a U-value of $4\ W/m^2°C$. To find one from the other we just divide it into 1. This is known as a reciprocal relationship.

With all materials, except air, resistance is proportional to thickness and the first column of Table 4.1 gives the thermal resistivity of various materials per millimetre of thickness. The resistance of air depends on other factors and can affect a structure in two areas.

Air spaces within a structure

Heat is transmitted across air spaces by radiation, conduction and convection. As the gap widens, conduction becomes more difficult but convection easier. After 25mm, as fast as the resistance increases because of poorer conduction, it is reduced by greater convection. There is therefore no advantage from a heat-loss point of view in having an air gap wider than 25mm. Table 4.2 gives air space resistances and the resistances of boundary layers.

Table 4.1 Thermal and vapour resistivity of building materials

	Thermal resistivity	Vapour resistivity
Structural		
Inner leaf brick	0.0016	0.030
Outer leaf brick	0.0012	0.030
Medium weight building block	0.0020	0.054
Light weight insulating block	0.0053	0.035
Cast dense concrete	0.0007	0.100
Granite	0.0004	0.300
Marble or slate	0.0005	DP
Sandstone	0.0008	0.150
Limestone	0.0007	0.200
Loose chippings	0.0010	N
Softwood	0.0077	0.045
Hardwood	0.0063	0.050
Rendering		
Asphalt surface	0.0020	DP
Exterior rendering	0.0020	0.100
Dense sand plaster	0.0020	0.060
Lightweight plaster	0.0050	0.050
Cladding		
Asbestos cement sheet	0.0028	0.002
Hardboard	0.0125	0.030
Plasterboard	0.0063	0.050
Plywood	0.0067	0.030
Chipboard	0.0067	0.060
Clay tiles	0.0012	0.030
Insulation		
Insulation board	0.0167	0.020
Glass fibre/mineral wool	0.0250	0.005
Expanded polystyrene	0.0286	0.200
U-foam	0.0250	0.025
Glass	N	DP
Polythene	N	DP

DP = damp-proof; N = Negligible in domestic thicknesses

Table 4.2 (a) Resistance of air spaces (m^2 °C/W)

Width (mm)	Heat flow up or horizontal		Heat flow down	
	Unlined	Aluminium-lined	Unlined	Aluminium-lined
5	0.10	0.19	0.11	0.18
6	0.11	0.21	0.12	0.23
7	0.12	0.23	0.13	0.28
8	0.13	0.25	0.14	0.34
10	0.14	0.27	0.16	0.40
15	0.16	0.30	0.18	0.61
20	0.17	0.33	0.20	0.83
25 and over	0.18	0.35	0.22	1.06

(b) Resistance of inside boundary layer (m² °C/W)

Structure	Heat flow direction	
Walls	Horizontal	0.12
Ceilings and floors	Upwards	0.10
Ceilings and floors	Downwards	0.14

(c) Resistance of outside boundary layer (m² °C/W)

Structure	Sheltered	Normal	Exposed
Walls	0.08	0.06	0.03
Roofs	0.07	0.04	0.02

Air boundary layers

Because of friction between the air and any surface, a thin, almost stationary, layer of air is held against the surface, which has a resistance to heat transfer. The resistance is less on outside surfaces because of wind movement and is less in windy exposed sites than sheltered ones.

Calculation of U-values

Using Tables 4.1 and 4.2 we can work out the U-value of most structures; a worked example of the method for a brick wall appears later.

Floors

Floors can have U-values worked out for them in the same way as walls and roofs but the floor does not lose heat evenly over its area. The ground beneath the floor tends to reach a steady temperature close to that of the house so that the main heat loss is from the edges. A large floor has a smaller ratio of edges to area than a small one.

Table 4.3 Floor U-values (W/m² °C)

Dimensions (metres)	Solid floors	Suspended wood floors
50 × 10	0.42	0.46
40 × 10	0.43	0.47
30 × 10	0.45	0.49
20 × 10	0.48	0.51
15 × 10	0.54	0.53
10 × 10	0.62	0.60
5 × 10	0.78	0.77
20 × 7.5	0.58	0.60
15 × 7.5	0.60	0.61
10 × 7.5	0.70	0.67
5 × 7.5	0.89	0.83
8 × 5	0.87	0.81
6 × 5	0.96	0.84
4 × 5	1.12	0.93

The above floor U-values are for four edges exposed; For three exposed edges values are 80 per cent (multiply by 0.80); For two exposed edges values are 60 per cent (multiply by 0.60).

In addition, not all houses are detached, with all four edges exposed. Table 4.3 gives U-values for different floor areas and a correction factor according to the number of edges exposed.

If your house is built on one continuous concrete slab which it shares with others, should you work to the overall U-value or the value for just the area you occupy? Generally it is better in the interests of accuracy to work to the value for your bit only. If you occupy the end house in a block of five, your floor will lose more heat than your neighbour's, who has only two edges exposed.

Most people in the trade work to a single U-value for floors regardless of size, mostly because they don't know of the variations and because the subject isn't mentioned in many books. The few who know do not think it worth bothering about, but they realize that the heat loss from the three walls of an end house is more than that from the two walls of a middle house. So why not allow for the third outside edge of the floor?

You may wonder if it is worthwhile using separate values for each room in a house. Usually it is not, because the areas are quite small and the rooms are interconnected so that temperatures tend to even out.

Temperature gradient

Where the temperature on one side of a structure is different from that on the other, there is said to be a temperature gradient and this varies in proportion to resistance. For instance, if one third of the resistance occurs across one section of a structure then one third of the temperature difference also takes place across that section.

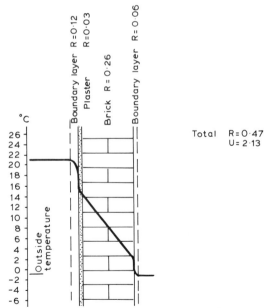

Fig. 4.1. Solid wall showing temperature changes through the structure. The mean temperature of the wall is about 8°C.

As an example, look at the cross-section of a solid brick wall in Fig. 4.1 from Table 4.1 the resistivity is 0.0012 °C m^2/W for each mm thickness (taking the outer leaf figure in this case). As it is 220mm thick, its resistance is 0.26 °C m^2/W (220 × 0.0012). The other resistances are totalled as shown.

The U-value of the wall is the reciprocal of the resistance of 0.47 which is 2.13 W/m²°C. The inside boundary layer resistance is 0.12°C m²/W, which is roughly 26 per cent of the total resistance of 0.47°C m²/W. Therefore approximately 26 per cent of the overall temperature difference will occur across the inside boundary layer. A quick way of getting the percentage as a decimal fraction is to multiply the component's resistance by the overall U-value. If this is multiplied by the overall temperature difference it will give the difference across the component.

If the temperature inside is 21°C and outside is −1°C, the difference is 22°C. To find the temperature difference caused by the inside boundary layer we multiply 0.12 (R) × 2.13 (U) × 22 (temp diff) = 5.62 °C. This means that the actual wall surface is at 15.38°C which is 5.62 °C lower than the inside temperature of 21°C.

The temperatures throughout the wall can be worked out and plotted on the cross-section against a temperature scale and then joined by a solid line. Typical temperature changes through a loft are shown in Fig. 4.2.

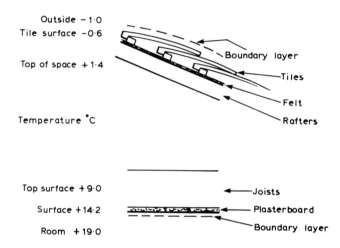

Fig. 4.2. Section through loft showing temperature variations

Vapour transmittance

In Table 4.1 there is another column giving vapour resistivity for the same materials. Where the letters 'DP' occur, these materials have very high resistances to the point where they can be considered damp-proof. Air can be taken as having no resistance to the passage of water vapour in the domestic environment, so we do not have to worry about the effect of boundary layers as we did with thermal transmittance.

As with thermal resistance, the figures are for a thickness of 1mm and should be multiplied by the thickness of the material to give the vapour resistance, which for comparison with thermal resistance I will call the VR of the material. When the component resistances are added together, they give the total VR of the structure in exactly the same way as thermal resistances add together to give the R value. Thermal transmittance (U-value) is the reciprocal of the thermal resistance (R). Similarly the vapour transmittance, which I call the VU-value, is the reciprocal of the vapour resistance (VR).

With thermal transmittance we are concerned with the difference in temperature between inside and outside: with vapour transmittance we are concerned with the difference in vapour pressure between inside and outside.

Vapour pressure is caused simply by one area having more moisture than another and whereas temperature is measured in degrees Centigrade, vapour pressure can be measured in Pascals, or Newtons/m^2 and millibars, and that's only the metric system. However, as I'm sure readers can more easily imagine moisture level as so many grams per cubic metre of air (g/m^3), I prefer to use this measure.

In a similar procedure to that for temperature differences, we find the vapour difference caused by each component by multiplying the component's vapour resistance by the VU-value of the whole structure and then by the overall vapour difference.

You will notice that generally substances with high thermal resistances have low vapour resistances. Glass-fibre insulation provides high thermal resistance, which means that it remains cold on its outer side. Unfortunately it has very little resistance to vapour which passes easily through to the cold side, where it condenses.

On the other hand polythene has no thermal resistance but enormous vapour resistance; it is the fact that the materials conflict in this way which causes all the trouble. However, if we know what we are doing we can use the different properties of materials to overcome the problem, which has become much more serious than it used to be.

5

Condensation

Old houses were very draughty: they had loose doors and windows, there was no felt under the slates. There was no hot water on tap, which meant that it had to be boiled over a fire and any steam went up the chimney as it did with cooking.

Compare that with a modern house. In order to save energy, as many cracks and gaps as possible are stopped up. There is felt under the slates or tiles and the loft is insulated, often preventing any air-flow through the loft. There is unlikely to be a chimney to carry any moisture away. There is hot water on tap and lots of it is used. Washing is done inside the house and cooking is done without a chimney.

The quantity of water that air is able to hold as an invisible vapour depends on temperature. Warm air might hold a large amount of water vapour which does no one any harm until it touches a surface which cools it to the temperature at which the vapour changes back into water; called the dew point.

Humidity and saturation

When air holds the maximum amount of water possible at a particular temperature it is said to be saturated. In order to measure different amounts of moisture present, a scale of humidity is used with perfectly dry air at zero humidity and saturated air at a relative humidity of 100; nowadays this is often quoted as a percentage.

Table 5.1 Saturated air (Relative humidity 100 per cent)

Air temperature (°C)	Moisture content (g/m³)	Air temperature (°C)	Moisture content (g/m³)
−5	3.26	10	9.44
−4	3.54	11	10.05
−3	3.83	12	10.70
−2	4.15	13	11.39
−1	4.50	14	12.12
0	4.87	15	12.89
1	5.22	16	13.69
2	5.58	17	14.53
3	5.97	18	15.42
4	6.39	19	16.37
5	6.83	20	17.36
6	7.29	21	18.40
7	7.78	22	19.50
8	8.30	23	20.65
9	8.86	24	21.86

Table 5.1 shows the maximum weight of water in grams that a cubic metre of air can hold at various temperatures. Air at 20°C, for instance, can hold a maximum of 17.36 grams per cubic metre (17.36 g/m³). If the air was 50 per cent saturated it would be holding 8.68 g/m³. If this air comes in contact with a window at 5°C then, from Table 5.1, the maximum that it could hold at this temperature would be 6.83 g/m³. As the air is holding more than that, some would be shed as condensation on the glass.

In winter the outside air can achieve up to 100 per cent humidity. When it enters the house, it is warmed and is able to hold more water. Each person contributes about 70 grams of water each hour from perspiration and breathing and this can treble with increased activity. Table 5.2 shows typical amounts of water put into the air by different activities.

Table 5.2 Moisture-creating activities

Washed clothes	*Water content in grams**
Shirt	100 to 200
Dress (cotton)	150 to 200
Dress (wool)	200 to 350
Towel	200 to 300
Blanket	700 to 1000
Bathing	*Evaporation in grams*
Quick bath	600
Long soak	1000
Cooking	*Evaporation in grams per hour*
Fast-boiling saucepan	1000
Simmering stock	500

* If spin-dried, content 60 to 90 per cent less

Condensation possibility

To give an idea of condensation potential consider a kitchen with solid walls, measuring 4m × 3m × 2.5m high. The inside temperature is 21°C and outside temperature −1°C with 85 per cent humidity. From Table 5.1, 100 per cent humidity would be 4.5 g/m³ at −1°C so at 85 per cent the air will hold 3.83 g/m³. The base level of humidity inside a house can be taken always as 2.0 g/m³ higher than outside before any moisture-producing activities take place so the base level indoors on this day will be 5.82g/m³.

A rapidly boiling saucepan can put a great deal of moisture into the air: a rate of 12 grams per minute is quite feasible. The volume of the room is 30 m³ and the saucepan is therefore increasing the humidity by 0.4g/m³ every minute. After five minutes the level will be increased from 5.83g/m³ to 7.83g/m³. If the window surface is at 6°C maximum humidity without condensation is 7.29g/m³ so condensation will start.

This type of wall will have a surface temperature of just over 15°C and condensation will occur when the moisture level is just over 12.89g/m³. If the water continues to boil away, condensation will appear on the walls after another 13 or 14 minutes.

Condensation may cause no harm if it runs down onto the window sill where it can be wiped off, but if it occurs on walls behind cupboards where it is not noticed there could be serious trouble.

Prevention of condensation

The three factors which cause condensation are high humidity, poor ventilation and low surface temperatures.

Humidity levels

We can reduce humidity by cutting out moisture-producing activities such as allowing saucepans to boil rapidly for long periods; this is also a waste of fuel and, if the water just simmers at boiling point, food cooks just as quickly, its value will be better and your kitchen will be drier.

Ventilation

For simplicity, I have ignored air changes in the kitchen so far. One air change per hour (30m³) would lengthen the time before condensation appeared on the walls to around 20 minutes. If the air change was increased to around 80 m³/h, by fitting an extractor fan, this larger volume of air would reduce the proportion of moisture and no condensation would occur on the wall. However, it would take an extraction of 200m³/h to lower humidity to the point where no condensation could appear on the window. This high rate of extraction would change the air around seven times an hour; think of the cost of heating that.

It is normal practice to allow for the air-change heat loss of a room when sizing the radiator for that room. However, if you think about it, with high extraction rates the kitchen air is replaced by already-warmed air from other parts of the house; that part of the radiator surface in the kitchen allowed to meet the air-change requirement is needed only when cold air is entering the kitchen from outside.

With an extractor fan the cold air enters the house in the other rooms and the radiators there have been sized to deal only with their respective room's estimated air-change loss; the extra cold air infiltration will not be allowed for and those rooms may be colder than expected.

This is not to say extractors should not be used; a little cooling in the house is preferable to the long-term effects of too much humidity and condensation, but extractors should be operated only when necessary. The ideal would be an extractor controlled by a humidistat, as heating is controlled by a thermostat.

Low surface temperatures

As window surfaces are at the lowest temperature and the first to collect condensation, this area causes most concern. However, condensation here is not very damaging; it can easily be removed and glass is not marked permanently as walls can be. In our kitchen example, double-glazing the window would raise its surface temperature from around 6°C to 13°C. The air could then hold a larger amount of moisture without condensing on the glass. However, the surface temperature of the wall is higher at around 15°C and if condensation occurs on the wall then it will still occur on the window. A general rule is that if, during cold weather, you regularly see condensation on your walls as well as windows then double-glazing will not cure any of it; no matter what the salesman says.

Moisture gradient

The difference in moisture level from one side of the structure to the other creates a moisture gradient just as the temperature difference creates a temperature gradient.

In the kitchen example, the actual moisture level which causes condensation on the wall is 13.19g/m³; the outside level is 3.83g/m³, which gives a difference of 9.36g/m³. The moisture difference, caused by each component, is calculated and, using these, the moisture levels at each interface can then be worked out.

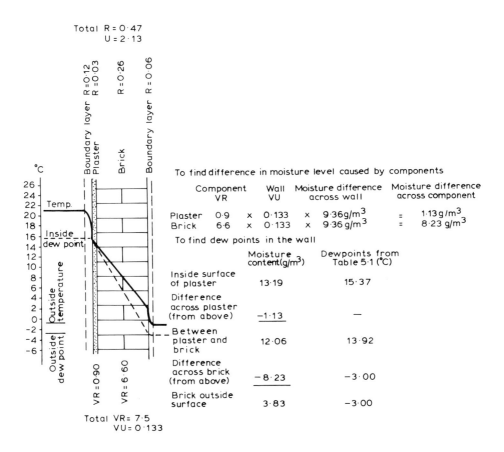

Fig. 5.1. Left: section through solid wall showing temperature gradient (solid line) and dewpoint gradient (broken line). On the right is method of finding moisture level at each interface in structure, and establishing of dew point temperatures for each moisture level

When we know the moisture content at each interface between components, we can use Table 5.1 to find the dew-point temperatures for each level. These can be plotted in the same way as the actual temperature, using a broken line, as in Fig. 5.1. If the solid line, representing actual temperature, is above the broken line, representing the dew point temperature, there will be no condensation. If the actual temperature line touches or is below the dew-point line, condensation will occur and if the actual temperature is very much below the dew point, there will be considerable condensation. In our example condensation just appears on the surface.

Condensation and insulation

Many householders suffering condensation on walls put insulation on the inside. This appears to be a better way of dealing with excessive humidity than high levels of extraction because it does not increase the heat loss, but actually reduces it. You are therefore killing two birds with one stone. You may also wreck your house.

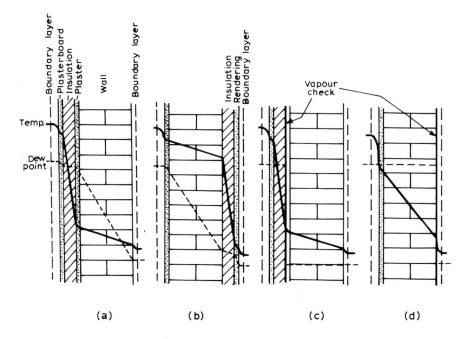

Fig. 5.2. At (a) the insulation has been put between the plaster surface and new plasterboard. The temperature drops rapidly and half-way through the insulation is below the dew point for the level of moisture present. Interstitial condensation will occur between this point and a point about 50 mm from outer surface. At (b) the insulation is on the outside and the U-value is the same as at (a). Because most of the temperature drop is on the outside of the structure, the moisture level and its dew point have had time to fall before this and nowhere is the temperature lower than the dew point and no condensation occurs. At (c) a vapour check has been put on the wall surface before insulating. This is a common mistake and, as the main temperature drop is on the inside, the temperature is below the dew point at the same position as with (a). At (d) a vapour check has been put on the outside to stop moisture penetrating. However, if the damp is caused by condensation from inside, this will cause interstitial condensation right through the wall

Effect of insulation

The most common method of insulating solid walls is to screw battens to the wall and clad with plasterboard over 50 mm of glass fibre, as in Fig. 5.2a. Insulation increases the surface temperature so no condensation will occur there. However, because the insulation prevents heat passing through, the actual temperature has already dropped below the dew point of the moisture level present only half-way through the insulation.

Only towards the outside of the wall is the temperature above the dew point again; this means that over the entire area of the wall, from 25mm inside the cladding until about 50mm from the outside, completely out of sight from both sides, condensation is forming. It will not harm the brick too much but the wood battens will rot and the glass fibre become a soggy mess; this will eventually work through to the surface. Condensation occuring within the structure in this way is called interstitial condensation.

Outside insulation

A layer of insulation can be put on the outside of the wall, as in Fig. 5.2b, to give the same U-value as with insulation on the inside so there is no advantage from a heat loss point of view.

However, there is a dramatic difference in the condensation profile. At no point will there be any condensation in the wall.

Quite often a householder will see damp effects on solid walls and conclude that this is penetrating from the outside. If the level of moisture inside is not high, such as in an unused bedroom, and the inside temperature fairly low, this may be true and remedies are available. On the other hand, in a room with a high humidity level, such as a kitchen with poor ventilation, and where temperatures are fairly high, the fault may be condensation not rain penetration.

If the householder assumed it was penetration and thus applied damp-proofing, the effect would be to allow the moisture level to build up from inside because there would be no connection between inside and outside air and no moisture from the high level inside could dissipate to the lower level outside. There would now be interstitial condensation right through the wall even without insulation inside. If insulation were applied to the inside, the wall would be even worse affected. If in doubt, always ask a reputable company to look at the problem and tell you the correct solution.

Vapour checks

Damp-proofing on the outside creates a check to vapour transfer coming from outside. If it is entering the structure from inside then it is obviously a good idea to put a vapour check, sometimes called a vapour barrier, on the inside.

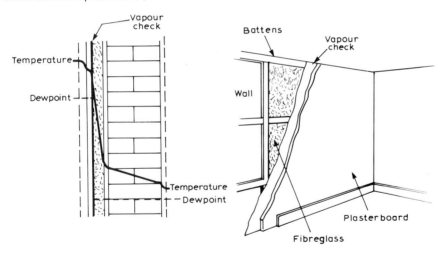

Fig. 5.3 Left: a cross-section showing the vapour check in its correct position as close to the warm side as possible. The temperature drops just as quickly through the insulation but the vapour check keeps the moisture level and hence the dew point low. No condensation will take place anywhere. Right: the method of insulating inside wall surfaces. Of course, other insulation can be used (such as polystyrene slabs), but the vapour check must be in the same relative position

A vapour check of polythene should be fixed to the battens and over the glass fibre, as in Fig. 5.3, before the plasterboard is put up. The temperature still drops rapidly from the inside surface, but it doesn't matter because no humid air is getting past the polythene. The only part of the wall that moisture reaches is the plasterboard but this is at too high a temperature for condensation to occur.

It is very important, when fitting a vapour check, that there are no gaps and that joins are made by folding over. Where holes have to be made for light switches etc., make them as small as possible. It is possible to buy plasterboard with aluminium foil on the back, which acts as a vapour check but is not as effective as carefully applied polythene. Fixing a vapour check adds very little to the time of the job and very little extra to the cost; it is asking for trouble to cut this corner.

Vapour checks should be fitted as close as possible to the warm humid side of the structure.

Lofts

Similar problems occur in lofts because insulation is applied just above the ceiling. The temperature drop through 100mm insulation is enormous with the result that the space above the insulation becomes much colder, as you can see by comparing Fig. 5.4 with Fig. 4.2. There is no way of fixing a vapour barrier short of taking all the ceiling down so nothing can prevent moisture-laden air from passing into the loft space. Once there it condenses on the cold surfaces, particularly the felt under the tiles, because not only is this very cold, it is a vapour check itself. It is a check in the right place for the days when all the damp came from outside but it's not in the right place for a well-insulated loft.

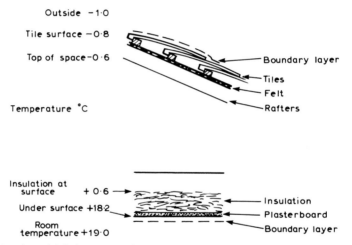

Fig. 5.4. Section through loft showing rapid temperature drop through insulation. Water pipes above the insulation will be near freezing with outside temperature of −1°C. Compare with loft in Chapter 4 where, at the same outside temperature, pipes above the ceiling would be at 9.0°C

Some people try to prevent glass fibre in the loft becoming wet due to condensation dripping from the felt by covering the insulation with polythene. This new vapour check would not only stop water getting down to the insulation, it would also prevent vapour from getting above the insulation and condensation would settle between the ceiling and the polythene, which could rot the joists.

In inhabited spaces it is better to deal with humidity without creating large air-change rates, because of the heat loss. In areas such as the loft the best way is to provide plenty of air movement.

The 1983 Building Regulations state the size of air space required in new buildings. If you live in a building which has loft insulation, ensure that the air flow is up to standard. The requirements are that a minimum 10mm gap should run along the eaves; this gap should allow air to pass through and it should not be further hindered by insulation or other materials, on its way into the loft space. Special eaves vents are available now to provide the gap and to retain the insulation.

In an existing property, where it is not possible to create the required 10mm gap, vents can be fitted into the soffit as in Fig. 5.5, or air bricks or ventilators can be fitted in opposite gable walls to give the same area as would have been provided by the 10mm gap along the eaves.

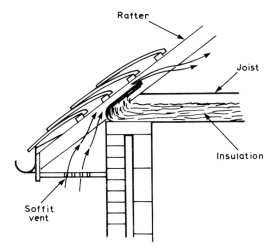

Fig. 5.5. Eaves vents for existing dwellings to bring up to Building Regulation standard. The one part is fitted from inside the loft and provides clear airways by restraining the insulation; the other part is fitted into holes cut in the soffit

Intermittent heating

All the above points relate to steady-state conditions, where the heating has been on for some time and the temperatures have stabilized. If the heating has been off for some time, it will take a time for the surfaces to reach the steady-state levels and condensation will start earlier.

Conclusions

The subject of condensation in domestic property is complex and insufficiently considered. Most builders and heating engineers have very limited knowledge — a large number do not even know there is a problem. To give some help to anyone wanting to reduce the potential hazard of condensation, here are some guidelines.

1.   A higher level of heating should be provided in humid areas such as bathrooms and kitchens, in order to create higher surface temperatures and so that the air can hold more moisture as vapour.

2.   In kitchens, food should be simmered rather than boiled rapidly, to cut down the 'steam'.

3.   The extraction of moist air from bathrooms and kitchens should prevent it reaching other parts of the house. The more moisture extracted here, before it reaches other parts of the house, the lower can be the temperatures in unused rooms mentioned in 5.

4.   To conserve heat, extractor fans should be capable of adjustment so that only sufficient air is removed to hold the moisture level low enough to avoid saturation of the air and consequent condensation.

5.   A certain amount of heat should be supplied to unused rooms.

6.   Condensation on windows provided it can be drained off will not do a lot of harm and double glazing may not cure it.

7.   Condensation in cupboards should be dealt with by increasing air flow through them by venting top and bottom near the wall.

8.   Condensation occurring on porous surfaces and able to evaporate or diffuse quickly will do very little harm.

9.   Moisture entering the structure should be able to evaporate from the outside surface. Damp-proofing of the outside surface, whether wall or roof, should be undertaken only in special circumstances.

10.   Interstitial condensation occurring only in the outside leaf of a cavity wall will cause no harm.

11.   Interstitial condensation in insulation and timber can cause severe rot and possible structural collapse.

12.   To prevent interstitial condensation, a vapour check must be placed over the whole area of any insulation and as close as possible to the warm side.

13.   Any condensation problems in lofts should be cured by a vigorous air flow being created.

6

The basic heating system

The basic principle of heating is very straightforward and is illustrated in Fig. 6.1. A certain quantity of water is heated at a boiler. The water is circulated in pipes to give up its heat through radiators or convectors and is returned to the boiler to be reheated.

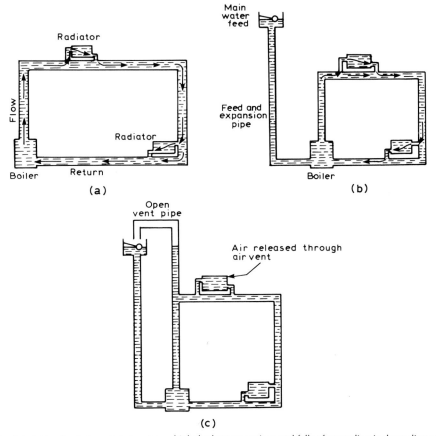

Fig. 6.1. (a) is a basic 'gravity' circuit in which the hot water rises and falls after cooling in the radiators. However, there is no means of filling. (b) has a means of filling and of accepting expansion in the shape of a feed and expansion cistern, but no way for air to escape. (c) is a complete workable system with safety vent pipe added. This is not the expansion pipe as it is often mistakenly called

In early systems circulation was by natural convection. When water is heated it becomes lighter and will rise naturally from the boiler. When water enters radiators it gives up its heat to the air via their large surface areas. As colder water is heavier it falls from the top connection on the radiator to the bottom opposite connection and eventually back to the boiler. This is known as gravity circulation. The top circuit connection at the boiler is called the flow and the bottom connection is the return.

The basic system as illustrated presents some practical difficulties. How do we get the water into the system and what happens when the water is heated and expands?

Feed and expansion cistern

The traditional method of dealing with filling and expansion is by the feed and expansion cistern. This is often called the feed and expansion tank, the header tank or the make-up tank, although strictly a tank is a closed vessel. The pipe connecting it to the system is called the feed and expansion pipe.

The cistern is supplied with water from the mains through a ball-valve. When the water reaches a pre-determined level, the valve is closed. The cistern must be the highest point of the system so that all parts can be filled from it.

When the water is heated, expansion can take place up the feed and expansion pipe and into the cistern. Because of this, the ball-valve is set to close when the cistern is only about one-third full, leaving a space to accept the expansion volume. If this space were not allowed, every time the water was heated it would overflow.

Providing a feed pipe enables us to accept expansion and to fill the system but it does not solve another problem. The system is full of air to begin with and the water cannot replace it if the air cannot escape. The answer is to provide another pipe through which the air can rise. This is known as the open vent or overflow pipe but, because of its very important other duty, it is best described as the open safety vent.

Other parts of the system which could trap air also need a venting facility. This is particularly true of radiators, which are supplied with air vents to be opened and closed by a vent key.

Safety

In the early boilers running on solid fuel, there was little control over the burning rate and occasionally the water boiled. This presented no danger because the open safety vent allowed the steam to escape. Modern boilers have thermostats which shut off the fuel supply in the case of oil and gas, or operate a damper or fan with solid fuel. With solid fuel there is always a delay and with other fuels there is always the possibility of a thermostat failing. It is vital therefore that the safety vent pipe offers an open and continuously-rising escape route for boiling water. There should be no valves, pumps or controls on this pipe.

If the boiling water vents safely, it must be renewed or the system will become overheated — and a boiled-dry boiler is more expensive to replace than a saucepan! It is therefore just as important that the feed and expansion pipe is also open to allow the replacement water to enter the system. In book after book, I find the pump is shown on this pipe and often other control valves; this should not be done. Circulation should never be restricted around the feed and expansion circuit.

Combined feed and vent

Sometimes what is called a combined feed and vent is fitted, as in Fig. 6.2. Notice that I do *not* refer to it as a combined feed and safety vent. This is because it isn't safe. If the water boils, it can vent through the vent pipe but replacement water cannot reach the boiler; it can't be going down while the boiling water is coming up.

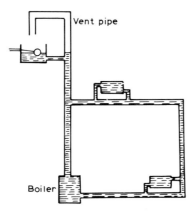

Fig. 6.2. A combined feed and expansion pipe and vent pipe, which illustrates the impossibility of venting steam and replenishing with replacement water at the same time

Pumps

We now have the basis of a heating system but the circulation is still by 'gravity', which depends on the difference in weight of water at different temperatures. The circulating pressure is very weak and the water moves slowly; large quantities of water are needed to carry the required heat and large-bore pipes are needed.

The rapid acceptance of domestic central heating in this country was due to the introduction of neat small pipework, the greater circulating pressure needed being provided by a pump. Much of the credit for this new small-bore heating belongs to the Coal Utilization Council, now the Solid Fuel Advisory Service.

Introducing a pump into the system improves circulation but creates some problems of its own due to the two types of pressure in a system.

Static pressure

In the basic arrangement there is a pressure caused by the weight of water over a given area, which in the old imperial terms could be measured in pounds force per square inch and now could be kilograms force per square metre. However, as the pressure over the unit area is proportional to the height of the water, it is convenient to refer to pressure in relation to the height, or head, of the water. The pressure exerted by this height when the system is at rest is called the static head.

Dynamic pressure

The pump moves water by creating a pressure difference; it pushes in one direction and pulls from the other. This pressure, unlike static pressure, is caused by movement and is known as dynamic pressure; it also can be expressed as a force exerted over an area. However, it is useful to refer to it in terms of height as with static head and it is generally referred to as pump head.

A pump might be said, for example, to deliver 2 litres of water per second with a head of 3m, which means it can lift water at that rate to that height. The volume of water needed depends on how hot it is so, before going more deeply into the system pressures, let us consider what temperatures we will need.

Measurement of heat

If we raise the temperature of 10 kilograms of water from 6 °C to 16 °C, a rise of 10 °C, a certain amount of energy will be held by the water, which can be given out as required. If we raise the temperature another 10 °C, to 26 °C, we have doubled the energy stored. Alternatively, we could heat a further 10 kilograms to only 16 °C to double the energy.

A large volume of water can be used at a low temperature or a small volume at a high temperature, both carrying the same amount of energy. The rate of heat transfer is proportional to difference in temperature so it is better to have as high a water temperature as possible.

It is impossible to heat above 100°C because the water would just boil away. In addition the surfaces of radiators would be dangerously hot to the touch. The highest temperature range that is practical and safe is around 75 °C to 85 °C.

Temperature drop

Because this country used to work in imperial units, the maximum flow temperature was set at 180 °F. As the water circulates around the system it gives up its heat at the emitters and so becomes cooler. The more it is allowed to cool, the more heat will be given up. But if it cools very much, the mean temperature in the circuit will be lower and larger emitters will be needed to obtain the same emission. The standard was set at a return of 160 °F giving a mean temperature of 170 °F.

The fall in temperature is called the temperature drop and was a convenient 20 °F. The result of metrication was that the converted temperature drop became 11.1 °C, being the difference between the straight conversions of 82.2 °C flow and 71.1 °C return. A more suitable drop would be 10 °C with a flow of 85 °C, a return of 75 °C and a mean of 80 °C. The new British Standard for radiator emissions is based on this and, as the boiler standard will no doubt follow, I will use a 10 °C temperature drop in all the calculations.

Quantity of water

The heat energy that water can hold is related to its mass, as with specific heat of building materials mentioned in Chapter 2, and strictly speaking we should refer to its mass in kilograms. However, as 1 litre of water has a mass of 1 kg at normal temperature and is only slightly lighter at circulating temperature, and as pump performance is always given using volume flow, it will make things easier to work in litres throughout.

The metric unit of energy is the joule but, unlike the old imperial British Thermal Unit, it is so small that most people avoid it. However, I mention it here to explain an odd number that we will need. It takes 4187 joules to raise the temperature of 1 litre of water by 1 °C; to raise the temperature by 10 °C would therefore need 41 870 joules. When the litre of water cools by 10 °C it gives up 41 870 joules.

A watt is defined as a rate of energy transfer of 1 joule per second so if the litre of water gives up its 41 870 joules in only one second, it is transferring heat at a rate of 41 870 watts.

From this you can see that if we divide the heating requirement in watts by 41 870, it will tell us how many litres must flow every second in our heating circuit. If the heat losses of your house amount to 167 480 watts, then dividing by 41 870 produces a requirement of 4 litres per second (4l/s). This flow rate must be supplied through pipework and the next thing is to find out what size will be needed.

Velocity

A 15mm diameter tube 1m long can contain 0.145 litres of water. If 4l/s are required, we need the water contained in 27.6 metres to flow every second; this means the water will be travelling at a speed of 27.6 metres per second or in more vivid terms 62 mph, which is a bit reckless around the house! In practice it is found that a velocity of 1 metre per second is as fast as you can go if vibration and noise are to be within acceptable limits.

As one metre of tube holds 0.145 litres, and we cannot exceed a velocity of 1m/s then 0.145 l/s is all we can push through this size of tube. If 1 l/s cooling 10 °C provides 41 780 watts, then 0.145 l/s will provide 6058 watts, which is the maximum heat load of 15 mm tube. Table 6.1 gives rounded limits for the other sizes of small-bore tube.

Table 6.1 Load and length limits of small-bore copper tube

Nominal diameter (mm)	Maximum load (watts)	Flow (l/s)	Length limits (m)
15	6 000	0.145	24
22	13 400	0.320	36
28	22 500	0.537	53

Friction

I said earlier that a pump's performance can be measured by reference to the water flow rate and the height to which it can be lifted. The pump's ability to lift water has many applications but in a heating system no lifting is necessary, since the circuit is already full of water held up by static pressure. The pump is needed to create a pressure differential to get the water moving and to overcome friction.

As water travels along a tube, friction exists between it and the tube walls. If there is twice the length of tube, there will also be twice the friction. If the same pump mentioned earlier, which can deliver 2 litres per second with a head of 3m, were to pump along a length of pipe and at the end, 2 l/s could be lifted to a height of only 2 m then the pump has lost 1 m of its head overcoming the friction in the pipe.

Put another way, this length of pipe, for a flow rate of 2 l/s, produces a head loss of 1 m. If the flow increases, the friction will increase. Table 6.2 shows the head loss, in milimetres, per metre run of pipework, for different sizes of tube at varying flow rates. As we use a standard 10 °C temperature drop, the heat carried is always proportional to the flow rate so I have shown the heat load in watts.

In a straightforward domestic system it is rarely necessary to use such a table but its use is explained in Chapter 12.

Fittings

The pressure-loss figures in Table 6.2 are for straight tubes. If there are fittings or valves along the length of tube, these will increase the friction. In the early days of 'gravity' systems and iron pipes, it was necessary to calculate the pressure loss caused by each fitting but in modern small-

Table 6.2 Resistance of copper tube at different load and flow rates

Load (watts)	Flow (l/s)	Millimetres head loss per metre run of tube			
		15 mm	22 mm	28 mm	35 mm
1 000	0.024	4			
1 500	0.036	8			
2 000	0.048	12			
2 500	0.060	18			
3 000	0.072	25	4		
3 500	0.084	33	5		
4 000	0.096	42	6		
4 500	0.108	52	8		
5 000	0.120	62	10		
5 500	0.132	74	12		
6 000	0.144	86	14	4	
7 000	0.168		17	5	
8 000	0.191		21	6	
9 000	0.215		26	7	
10 000	0.239		32	9	
11 000	0.263		38	11	4
12 000	0.287		44	13	5
13 000	0.311		51	15	5
14 000	0.335			17	6
15 000	0.359			19	6
16 000	0.383			21	7
17 000	0.407			24	8
18 000	0.431			26	9
19 000	0.455			29	10
20 000	0.479			31	11
21 000	0.503			34	12
22 000	0.527			37	13
23 000	0.551				14
24 000	0.574				15
25 000	0.598				17
26 000	0.622				18
27 000	0.646				19
28 000	0.670				20
29 000	0.694				21
30 000	0.718				23
31 000	0.742				24
32 000	0.766				25
33 000	0.790				27
34 000	0.814				28
35 000	0.840				30

Pump head losses are often shown as pressure loss in pascals or newtons/m^2, which are the same. To convert the head loss in milimetres per metre run shown above, multiply by 9.807 or, for a quick approximation, by 10.

bore systems it is usual just to add a percentage to the length. For compression fittings we add 35 per cent and for capillary we add 30 per cent.

For example, in a length of 30 m with an average number of capillary fittings along it we would say the fittings create a pressure-loss equivalent to another 9 m of clear pipe. The actual length of 30 m with fittings is equivalent to a plain length of 39 m.

All pumps have a performance graph which indicates what they can do. You can see, from the typical one depicted in Fig. 6.3, that as head loss caused by friction increases, the flow rate that the pump can deliver decreases.

At the maximum flow rate for 15 mm tube of 0.145 l/s, Table 6.2 indicates a head loss of 86 mm per metre run. A run of 24 m will create a head loss of 2064 mm or just over 2 m. If the tube length is doubled the friction and head loss will double to just over 4 m.

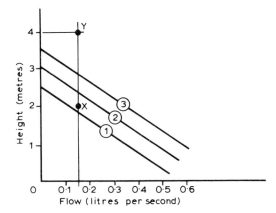

Fig. 6.3. A pump graph. Point 'X' represents a heating circuit with a flow requirement of 0.145 ℓ/s and a head loss of 2 m, which is within the pump's capacity. Point 'Y' represents a circuit with the same flow needs but with twice the resistance and head loss; this is above the performance line and would be too much for the pump

The load-carrying limits in Table 6.1 are caused by speed restrictions and obviously these limits are reduced further if there is excessive friction caused by very long lengths. The limits in Table 6.1 can be used if the lengths do not exceed those shown at the foot of the table. However, there is not much to worry about because it is very unlikely that these lengths will be exceeded in domestic heating.

Pump position

In Fig. 6.4, the open safety vent is only 1.4 m above point 'X'; it also has some frictional resistance but together the vent pipe offers less resistance than the 2.3 m of the heating circuit and water will be pumped up and over this easier path.

Although in theory we could put a restrictor valve on the vent pipe to increase its resistance and force the water around the heating circuit, we must not restrict this pipe for safety reasons. The next idea might be to increase the height of the vent pipe but if the heating circuit had a very

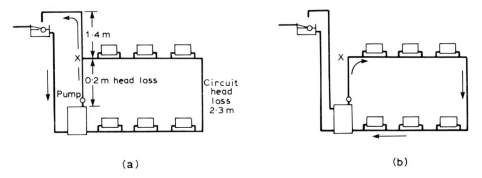

(a)   (b)

Fig. 6.4. At (a) pump has sufficient power to overcome 2.3 m head loss in circuit. If head loss from boiler to point 'X' is 0.2 m then 2.1 m of head loss remains in circuit. With vent only 1.4 m high, water will prefer this easier route. Diagram (b) has feed and expansion pipe and safety vent pipe on same side of pump and little pressure difference between them

high resistance, say with microbore tube, it might be necessary to increase the height by 2 m or 3 m and it would be poking through the roof. Obviously another solution must be found.

Where the open safety vent is on the opposite side of the pump to the feed pipe, it is possible for water to be pumped up the vent pipe and pulled down the feed. If both pipes were on the same side of the pump this could not happen and a simple way of achieving this is to connect the vent pipe to another tapping on the boiler. It will then be impossible for the water to circulate around these pipes and we don't have to worry about the height of the vent and the problems of aeration caused by pumping over.

With a pump in the circuit we are not relying on movement caused by natural convection and the flow connection to the radiator does not need to rise to the top as in a 'gravity' system, which is why many modern radiators do not have any top tappings at all.

Pump in return

For many years the preferred pump position was in the return to the boiler. In fact, boilers supplied with the pump already fitted had it on the return. From a circulation point of view, this makes no difference because the heating circuit is receiving the same pump pressure. This position, however, has disadvantages due to the heating circuit being on the negative side of the pump. These disadvantages have only become real problems with the introduction of high-resistance low-water-content boilers but, as these are very popular, avoiding these problems is very important and this is where we look more closely at the pressures in a system caused by the pump.

7

Circuit hydraulics

A pump circulates water by creating a pressure differential but it does not remove or introduce water. Therefore any water it moves into one part of the circuit it must obtain from somewhere else. What it pushes out of its 'positive' side it pulls in to its 'negative' side.

   If a pump is put into the base of a simple open U-tube as in Fig. 7.1 and it has sufficient head to cause a 4 m differential then, when it is switched on, the column of water, which we will call A, on the positive side will be pushed up 2 m and column B on its negative side will be pulled down 2 m. The difference in height between the columns is the 4 m differential.

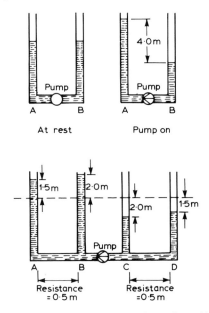

Fig. 7.1. Top: U-tube illustrates effect of 4 m head pump. Below: effect of frictional head loss in pipework, on height of each column

   If we take another horizontal pipe from each side to connect two more vertical pipes as illustrated and each horizontal pipe produces friction equal to a 0.5 m head loss, the outer column A on the positive side will rise only 1.5 m; the outer column D on the negative side will fall an equal 1.5 m. The difference in height between these two is 3 m because a total of 1 m of the pump head has been used to overcome the two horizontal resistances of 0.5 m.

We can extend this arrangement and then join the ends to create a continuous circuit such as in Fig. 7.2. When the pump is on, the levels alter: those on the positive side of the pump rise and those on the negative side fall. Half-way around the circuit the positive pressure balances the negative pressure and there is no change in height. This is known as the neutral point.

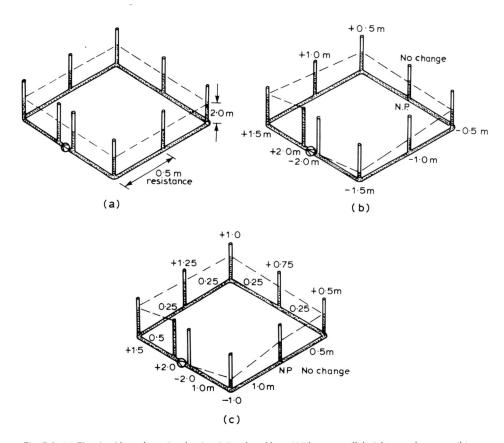

Fig. 7.2. (a) Circuit with each section having 0.5 m head loss. With pump off, heights are the same. (b) Same circuit with pump on. The various heights are shown joined by broken line. (c) Circuit has uneven distribution of the pipe resistances but neutral point is still at mid point in relation to them, having 2 m resistance on each side. However, its physical position is closer to the pump

If the circuit is made up of eight sections each having a resistance equal to a head loss of 0.5 m, there will be a total resistance of 4 m. If this total resistance were not in equal portions around the circuit, the neutral point would move farther from or nearer to the pump. But, wherever it moves from a physical position point of view, it is always at the half-way point in relation to the resistance.

At this neutral point the static pressure is the same whether the pump is on or off. On the positive side of the pump the water levels increase by varying amounts, each of which represents the pump pressure available at that point. Because the heights are greater on the positive side, the static pressure at the base of each column is greater by the amount of each increase. On the negative side of the pump the levels are reduced and the static pressure is reduced.

The term 'neutral point' means a point where there is no change in the static pressure. Of course, in a normal heating system you don't have all these open pipes; there are only two, the feed and expansion pipe and the open vent pipe.

Effect of feed and expansion pipe and open vent pipe

In order to show the effect of the feed and expansion cistern, let us go back to the original simple U-arrangement but this time we will give tube B three times the area of tube A, as in Fig. 7.3.

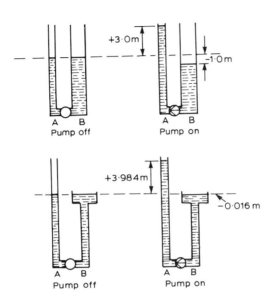

Fig. 7.3. Top: U-tube illustrates what happens when column B has three times the area of column A. The difference in height maintained by the pump remains at 4 m but it is not equally shared by both columns. Below: with a cistern at B of 249 times the area of tube A the level will drop 0.016 metres in B and rise 249 times this in tube A. The differential is still the 4 m head of the pump

   If the water in A rose 2 m, that in B could not fall 2 m because the water pulled from tube B will have three times the volume of the water needed to increase the height in A by 2 m. The heights will adjust automatically. Column B would fall 1 m and column A would rise three times this i.e. 3 m. The differential is still 4 m.
   If a cistern is fitted to the top of tube B with a surface area 249 times that of tube A (the odd number is only to avoid long decimal fractions in the text), whatever volume is pushed up into column A from column B will cause an increase in height of 249 times the reduction in height of the cistern water. But with the same 4 m head pump, the difference in height must remain at 4 m. If B is pulled down 0.016 m the volume of this thin slice off the top of the cistern water will occupy 3.984 m of the narrow tube A. The difference between the two heights is held at 4 m.
   As you now know, the static pressure at any point depends on the height of the water above it. If the height of the water in the cistern hardly alters then the static pressure at the foot of column B hardly alters. Because of the very small change in pressure this point has traditionally been treated as the neutral point. This may have caused some confusion but let's go along with it.
   For circulation to take place, a pressure differential must exist between different points so you cannot have a circuit with two neutral points because no circulation could take place between them. Therefore, if the neutral point is where the feed and expansion cistern joins the circuit, that is the one and only neutral point and pressures around the circuit must adjust to this.

Circuit pressures with feed and expansion cistern

A combined feed and open vent pipe should not be fitted but to illustrate a point let us consider a combined feed and vent connecting the cistern to the circuit at the natural neutral point, as in Fig. 7.4. As there cannot be any pressure difference between the feed pipe and the vent pipe, because they are one and the same where they join the circuit, there can be no movement of water between them. The height of the water in the cistern stays at the same level as when the pump is off and the point where the combined feed and vent joins the circuit will be a genuine neutral point.

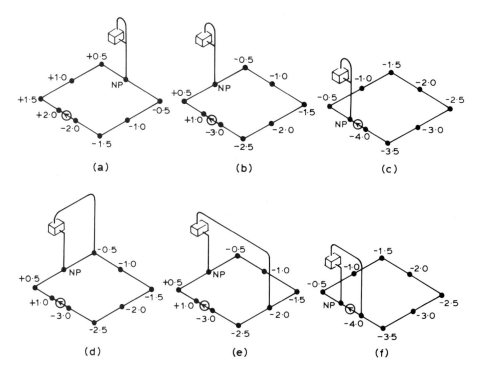

Fig. 7.4. The total resistance of all circuits is 4 m made up of eight sections each of 0.5 m head loss. Diagram (a) shows combined feed and vent at normal neutral point. Wherever the connection is made as in (b) and (c), this is always the neutral point because no change in level can possibly occur; the pressures around the circuit will adjust to this but always keeping in the same relationship to the resistances. When there are two points open to the atmosphere, levels change in proportion to the difference in pressure at each point. As the cistern now is on the positive side of the pump and the vent on the negative side, the level of the cistern will rise and that in the vent will fall. At (d) the difference can only be 0.5 m, at (e) it is 2 m and at (f) it is the full 4 m of the pump head. In each case, with a cistern area 249 times the vent area, the level in the cistern will rise 1/249 of the fall in the vent. The true neutral point is where no change in pressure occurs and is just a little way from the cistern connection, towards the vent

If the cistern is connected at any point, no change in the level of the cistern occurs because there is no other place which could accept or supply the water caused by any change. Note that as the cistern is moved closer to the positive side of the pump, the positive pressure reduces because it is needed only to overcome the resistance between the pump and neutral point. As the distance and the resistance increase on the negative side of the pump, more negative pressure is used.

Of course this combined feed and vent breaks the safety rule because these two pipes should be completely separate. If we separate them and put the vent at a point of 0.5 m negative pressure and the cistern area is, as before, 249 times the area of the open vent pipe then, from what has been covered so far, because the vent is now on the negative side of the pump, its level will fall and the level in the cistern will rise one 249th of this — a negligible amount.

But the vent could be connected at a point where its water level would fall much more. In the worst case it will fall almost 4 m or, to be exact, it will fall 3.984 m and the cistern level will rise 0.016 metres. If the cistern level rises by even this small amount, then where it connects is not the neutral point; it is, in fact, a point where the positive pressure can sustain a head of 0.016 m. The real neutral point is somewhere between the vent and this 'not quite the neutral point'.

This may seem hardly worth talking about but, because of the large area of the cistern, this tiny increase in height can have an enormous effect when the volume necessary for it is drawn from a narrow vent pipe somewhere else in the circuit. The vent water level can be reduced to the point where air is pulled into the system.

The opposite effect occurs when the feed and expansion cistern is connected to the negative side of the pump and the vent to the positive. In this case water will rise some distance up the vent which is all right if the vent is high enough. If it is not, the water flows out of it into the cistern and we have circulation around the feed and expansion circuit.

To keep the change in the water level to a minimum, the feed and expansion pipe and the open vent must be connected to the circuit as close as possible so that there will be very little circulating pressure between them. The only place where this can be done, which also allows each pipe to have an unrestricted safety route from the boiler to the cistern, is at the boiler itself, leaving the heating circuit alone with the full head of the pump. This is easily arranged by having two tappings on the boiler for the heating circuit and two for the feed and expansion circuit, as in Fig. 7.5. This has worked perfectly in the past but now newer types of boiler have only two tappings, which I will deal with later.

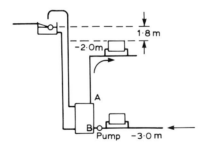

Fig. 7.5. With a pump on the return, a negative pressure can be produced at the radiators, which may be more than the height of water in the vent; this will cause the pressure to fall below static pressure at the radiator and air may become entrapped

As the two open pipes are connected to the boiler on the same side of the pump, this makes the boiler the neutral point of the system. The level of water in the cistern and the vent pipe will hardly change regardless of where the pump is placed on the heating circuit, so it looks as though we can put the pump where we like. But there are other considerations.

Negative pump pressure

When the neutral point is close to the positive side of the pump, as it is when the pump is on the return pipe near to the boiler, most of the pump pressure will be negative. If, for instance, there were a pressure of minus 3 m on the suction side of the pump, there might be minus 2 m at an upstairs radiator as shown in the illustration.

Remember that a negative pump pressure reduces the static pressure accordingly; the static pressure at the radiator therefore will be 2 m less than with the pump off. If the cistern level is only; say, 1.8 m higher than the radiator, the level of water would fall 0.2 m in the radiator if it were open to the atmosphere. At this point you may say that the radiator is not open to the atmosphere nor is there an open vent pipe connected to it and, if air cannot get in to take the place of the water, the water level will not fall. You would be quite right in a perfect world but in reality it is almost impossible to obtain a hermetically sealed circuit.

There are always small gaps at joints and air vents, which allow air to pass. They are not large enough to allow water through because it is much 'thicker' than air and so they are never noticed but, whenever the pump is switched on, minute amounts of air are sucked into the system and collect at radiators. When this keeps happening some people increase the pump head 'to clear it out'. This makes things worse because the negative pressure is increased and draws in more air.

Apart from the fact that if sufficient air is drawn in to form an air lock, circulation will stop, there are other damaging effects, which I will go into later.

The ideal place for the pump is on the flow pipe so that the heating circuit is affected by positive pressure. The worst that could happen is that some water might be forced out of less-than-perfect joints when first commissioned but they could be tightened easily or re-made and that would be the end of it.

Single opening to atmosphere

When the cistern was connected to the circuit by a combined feed and vent, we saw that the point of connection was a true neutral point and no change in water level occurred. The combined feed and vent is not safe, and it is the separating of these two pipes for safety reasons which causes all the trouble with pressure differences.

If we could have a single opening to the atmosphere, as with the combined feed and vent, but with full safety provision we would have the best of both worlds. The whole system would be hydraulically stable and most of the problems of modern systems would disappear.

A device called the 'Spartan' accomplishes this. It is a copper vessel which is connected between the boiler and the vent and connecting to the cylinder and thus to the storage cistern. An air lock separates the heating water from the cylinder but the device can cope with any overheating or boiling with safety. The product has been tested on housing sites for around 10 years but is not widely known.

Golden rules

In a normal system where the two pipes are separated, to ensure that a system will perform properly and safely over a long period, without problems, there are three golden rules to follow:

1.   The feed and expansion pipe and the open safety vent should have unrestricted clear runs between the boiler and the feed and expansion cistern.

2.   There should be negligible pressure difference between the feed and expansion pipe and the open safety vent.

3.   The heating circuit should be under positive pressure.

8

Circuit variations

To make the diagrams simpler and demonstrate the pressures more clearly, the circuits so far illustrated have employed a single loop of pipe to circulate the water. This type of circuit is known as a one-pipe circuit; it has been used for years and may still be suitable in some cases.

One shortcoming is that after the first radiator on the circuit has emitted heat from the circulating water, the cooler water is returned to the main circuit; the next radiator therefore receives colder water than the first and so on. The first radiator will receive water at around boiler flow temperature and cool it slightly; the last radiator will be receiving water only just above boiler return temperature.

The mean temperature in each radiator will vary up to 10 °C. Each radiator temperature has to be separately calculated and the size adjusted for the different levels.

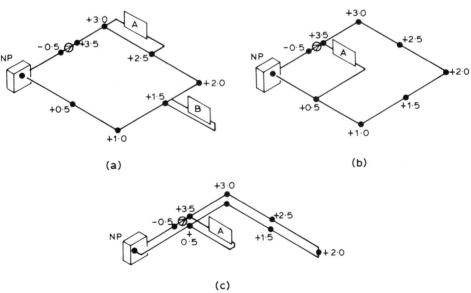

Fig. 8.1. Circuit (a) is a one-pipe loop with the same 0.5 m resistance in each section as before. With the feed and expansion pipe and vent pipe both connected to the boiler this is effectively the neutral point and the pressures with a 4 m head pump will be as shown. Radiator (A) would have a pressure difference of 0.5 m (between +2.5 m and +3.0 m). Radiator (B) would have very little pressure differential if connected to such close points. Circuit (b) has radiator (A) 'short-circuiting' the loop and the pressure difference is 3.0 m (+3.5 m and +0.5 m). Circuit (c) is closed up so that points of differing pressure are close together. Radiator (A) has a differential, as in circuit (b), of 3 m of head

47

Another weakness is that the closer points are situated on a one-pipe loop, the smaller the pressure difference between them. Radiator flow and return connections are close to each other as in Fig. 8.1, and because there is little difference in pressure the water may 'prefer' the lower resistance of the circuit pipe and bypass the radiator. To encourage the water to flow through the radiators it is sometimes necessary to increase the resistance of the main circuit where it passes below the radiator.

Two-pipe circuits

If we connected radiators to points on opposite sides of the loop, there would be much greater pressure differentials which would ensure good flow through the radiators. However, we can't connect every radiator across the loop circuit, as there would be chaos under the floorboards.

If we change the shape of the loop by pushing one side close to the other we can 'short-circuit' the loop from connecting points with high-pressure difference but which are physically close and this gives us a two-pipe circuit.

In the two-pipe circuit no radiator receives water which has been cooled by passing through another radiator first. The advantage of this is that the flow temperature to each radiator is close to the boiler flow temperature and each radiator return is close to the boiler return temperature. If each radiator in effect straddles these mains, then the mean temperature will be the same in each radiator and it makes sizing of radiators easier.

Provision of hot water

Until the 1920s most houses were provided only with cold water supply. When hot water was needed it was heated in kettles etc.

When bathrooms began to appear in dwellings, there was a need for hot water some distance away from any fireplace. There were two ways of providing this. In the first method gas water heaters called 'geysers' were fitted in the bathroom; these were about the size of a modern hot-water cylinder and their performance was unpredictable. Today unit heaters which heat water at the point of use are fitted in kitchen sinks etc., but they heat the water continuously as it is drawn off.

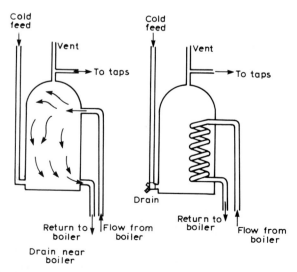

Fig. 8.2. On the left a direct cylinder; the water from the boiler is the same that reaches the taps. The indirect cylinder on the right separates the boiler water from the tap water

The second way was to put a copper back-boiler behind the fire and run pipes to a hot water tank or cylinder. The water drawn off at the taps circulates through the boiler. This is a direct system and works quite well because there is no steel in the system that could be corroded by the continual fresh water being introduced. There are many thousands of these systems in existence using a direct cylinder, illustrated in Fig. 8.2.

Occasionally a small radiator would be connected to the circuit to give heat in the bathroom; this would also be of copper. With full central heating it is too expensive to use copper throughout and so cast-iron boilers and cast-iron or steel radiators were fitted. These could be corroded by the action of continually supplied fresh water so the heating circuit and the hot water circuits were separated.

The hot water is heated indirectly in an indirect cylinder (Fig. 8.2). If the water in the heating circuit is never changed, there will be hardly any corrosion. As the hot water circuit is completely separated from the heating circuit, it cannot be filled from or vent to the same cistern and so it must have its own storage cistern and its own feed pipe and open vent pipe.

In a combined heating and hot water system there are three named circuits: the heating circuit, the primary circuit from the boiler to the cylinder and the hot-water supply circuit, called the secondary circuit.

Gravity

As explained in Chapter 5, the first heating systems employed 'gravity', and of course the circulation to the cylinder worked in the same way. When pumps and small-bore circuits were introduced, it was realized that if the pump was switched on or off either by a thermostat or a time-switch, the heating would be controllable.

If the primary circuit to the cylinder were also pumped, then it would go on and off according to the heating requirement, and in summer the heating would be off all the time. It was decided that it would be better if the primary circuit remained as a 'gravity' circuit, which meant retaining larger-bore pipes.

Vent and feed in combined systems

As mentioned earlier in Chapter 5, it is best to have the vent pipe and the feed pipe on the same side of the pump. In a combined system, there is a simple way of achieving this. As the primary circuit is a 'gravity' circuit without a pump on it, then using the feed pipe part way as the return from the cylinder and the vent pipe as the flow to the cylinder does not affect the important safety requirement of having these pipes clear (Fig. 8.3).

Between the boiler and the cylinder the sizes of the pipes depend on the hot water requirement and how much energy will need to be carried in the pipes. Table 12.11 (Chapter 12) will enable you to choose the correct size. Above the cylinder, the pipes can revert to the sizes for a normal feed pipe and safety vent pipe, which is 22mm in most domestic systems.

Fully pumped systems

Recent developments in boiler design have provided gas boilers with lower water content. These boilers are lighter and smaller than traditional boilers and can be hung on the wall. However, the small amount of water in the boiler cannot absorb the energy from the burners without boiling. It must therefore be constantly replaced and the water in the system must be kept moving. In this situation it is not possible to use a 'gravity' circuit and so the primary circuit must also be pumped.

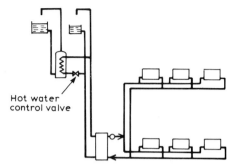

Fig. 8.3. Straightforward arrangement of pipework in a combined heating and hot water system. As the two circuits are separated, each must have its own means of filling, expanding and venting so two cisterns are needed

With the cylinder on a pumped circuit it is no longer possible to use the primary pipes as feed pipe and vent pipe and so the cylinder is treated like a radiator and placed on the heating circuit. The pipes are sized according to the cylinder requirement. As the pump is now affecting the cylinder as well as the heating circuit, it is no longer possible to control the heating separately by switching the pump on and off.

Control must be by a motorized valve on the cylinder circuit and another on the heating circuit as in Fig. 8.4. As we want to keep the feed pipe and the vent pipe on the same side of the pump and to keep them unobstructed, they cannot now share the primary circuit pipes and must be separated.

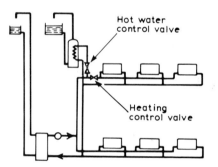

Fig. 8.4. With a fully pumped system, the cylinder is treated as a radiator but as its control needs to be different from the heating circuit, it needs a separate motorized valve

Caution. Solid-fuel boilers should not be installed with fully pumped circuits. A solid-fuel boiler, even one with electric fan and/or damper control, cannot be switched off instantly. There must always be a 'gravity' route for excess heat to be dissipated to the cylinder, when the pump is off.

Low-water-content circuits

The boiler bypass

A disadvantage of low-water-content boilers is that when the system is shut down and the burners go off, there is still enough residual heat to boil the small volume of water present. The water must be kept circulating for a while until the boiler cools down so a delay is arranged

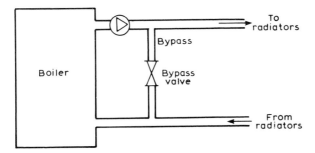

Fig. 8.5. With a low-water-content boiler the water must circulate for a little while after the heating and hot water circuits are satisfied, to prevent overheating. For this a bypass is fitted and, to prevent circulation through this when one of the circuits is calling for heat, its resistance is increased to slightly more than the highest head circuit (usually the heating circuit) by means of a bypass valve

before the pump stops, but if the heating and hot water circuits are closed, where can the water circulate? For this a bypass is fitted (Fig. 8.5).

The bypass circuit is short and has very little resistance so that when the other circuits call for heat, the water might flow around the bypass instead. To prevent this, a bypass valve is fitted. The valve must be closed sufficiently to force the water to flow around the proper circuits when they want heat but not so much that it reduces circulation through the boiler when the main circuits are closed.

Pump over-run

If the water is to continue circulating through the bypass and boiler after the burners have been shut off, the pump must run on for some time afterwards. To ensure this over-run, the boiler has a special delay timer built in to its electrical circuit. It is vital therefore that the pump and any thermostats are wired to the boiler junction box according to the maker's instructions; the pump must not be connected independently of the boiler wiring.

Boilers with two tappings

If we try to follow the basic system arrangement of connecting the feed and expansion pipe and the open safety vent pipe to the flow and return to the cylinder, we will end up with an arrangement similar to that in Fig. 8.6a which breaks two of the golden rules. Rule 1 is broken because the pump is situated in the open safety vent route and Rule 2 is broken because there is a large pressure difference between the safety vent pipe and the feed and expansion pipe. This type of boiler has a much higher resistance than a traditional boiler so, with the boiler resistance on one side and the heating circuit on the other, the vent pipe and the feed pipe are, from a pressure standpoint, on opposite sides of the circuit.

If the circuit is planned for safety, and both the safety vent pipe and the feed pipe offer clear separate routes between the boiler and the feed and expansion cistern as in Fig. 8.6b, Rule 2 is broken because of the pressure differential remaining in the feed and expansion circuit and we run the risk of circulation in this circuit.

Putting the pump in the return, as in Fig. 8.6c, does not change the pressure difference between the safety vent and the feed pipe and it also breaks Rule 3 because the heating circuit is now under negative pressure. The higher resistance of these boilers, together with smaller modern fittings and microbore, mean higher head pumps are required and the problems caused by negative pressure will be even greater.

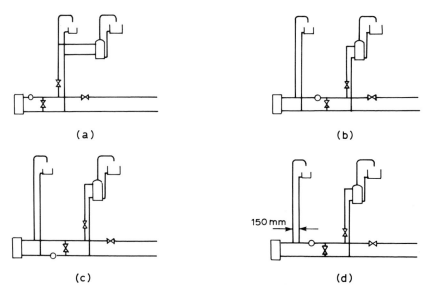

Fig. 8.6. (a) With the feed and expansion cistern connected like this, water will be pumped over because the feed pipe and the vent pipe have a large pressure differential between them. Also the pump is between the boiler and the cistern. (b) For safety the vent pipe can be connected between the boiler and the pump but the pressure differential is large and circulation around the feed and expansion and vent-pipe circuit will be encouraged. (c) With the pump on the return, the pressure differential is still great but it will have the opposite effect and air will be sucked down the vent pipe. (d) A close-coupled arrangement suitable for high hydraulic resistance boilers because there is very little pressure differential between the two pipes. They must not be connected farther than 150 mm apart. There is a direct vent route but replacement water has a tortuous route around the heating circuit before it can reach the boiler. This circuit arrangement must only be used with boilers having a high-limit thermostat

To minimize the negative pressure on the open safety vent, most manufacturers of these boilers suggest a close-coupled arrangement as in Fig. 8.6d, and to ensure a minimum pressure differential between the safety vent and the feed pipe, they recommend that the two pipes are connected close to each other (within 150 mm). The vent pipe is now under slight positive pressure and the pressure differential between it and the feed pipe is very small but Rule 1 is now broken.

The close-coupled feed and vent arrangement is almost a combined feed and vent. However, there is an unobstructed vent route from the boiler to the cistern but the route for replacement water goes all round the heating or bypass circuit, both of which have valves and a pump restricting free flow.

To cover this point, these boilers are fitted with a second thermostat called a high-limit stat. When this is done the manufacturers claim it is as safe as any other system complying with the first golden rule. They say that in addition to the extra thermostat there is still an open vent and a sort of replacement route.

This arrangement appears in British Standard 5449 and is accepted by gas boards but many installers and consultants are not completely happy with it. By understanding the circuits in some detail, you will be able to avoid the problems which can occur with these boilers.

Sealed-system circuits

The static pressure in a system is provided by the height of the feed and expansion cistern. If you have a flat-roofed house or a flat, it will not be possible to place the feed and expansion cistern high enough. In this case a sealed system can be considered. These systems are more common on the continent and in Canada and the USA than here.

The normal system is called 'closed' because once filled there should be very little intake of fresh water. However, it is still open to the atmosphere and subject to atmospheric pressure. The sealed system is entirely sealed from atmospheric pressure, and instead of the static pressure being provided by a high cistern it is provided by a pressure vessel as in Fig. 8.7.

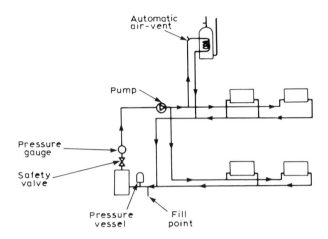

Fig. 8.7. A sealed system showing the basic requirements of pressure vessel, pressure gauge, safety valve and automatic air vents at high points. In addition some systems may need high pressure release valve, low pressure release valve and air separators.

Creating the pressure

The system water fills one side of the pressure vessel and air or a suitable gas at a set pressure fills the other side; between the two there is a flexible membrane. The pressure is usually set to be similar to that created by a cistern in a reasonably high loft.

In the conventional system, the water expands into the feed and expansion cistern; in a sealed system, the water expands into the vessel and compresses the gas. The compressed gas now exerts a greater pressure on the water.

The sealed system requires a number of extra items: a pressure relief valve to prevent the pressure becoming too great and a sensor for when the pressure becomes too low. When the system is first filled, the water displaces air; in a traditional system this is no problem as we have seen but the sealed system is closed to the atmosphere so careful attention must be paid to the means by which the displaced air can escape. Air is also released when water is heated and this must be catered for.

There are discussions at present on how a code of practice can be established but there are many different views on the standards to be set for sealed systems. The water boards are not greatly enamoured of the idea and the attitude of different authorities varies. If you ever contemplate a sealed system, the attitude and requirements of your water board and the local authority should be considered.

Because of the poorer control of temperature on solid-fuel boilers, these cannot be used with a sealed system. Many gas and oil-fired boilers are also unsuitable for sealed systems. Check first!

High temperatures

With a traditional system, the water boils at the usual 100 °C. If the pressure in a sealed system is increased to create a static head higher than normal, the water can become much hotter before it boils. We could have a system with the water at 120 °C.

The emission from radiators depends on the difference in temperature between the water and the air in the room. If the difference increases, the emission increases. With a higher water temperature we could increase the emission from radiators, which would mean smaller radiators for the same job. However, the present temperature is about as hot as we want if we are to avoid burning ourselves on the radiator surface. The only emitters which could take advantage of the higher temperature would be skirting heating.

A popular fallacy is that because smaller emitters are possible with sealed systems running at higher temperatures, these systems are more efficient. However, the energy required from the emitter is the same; we merely have a smaller volume at a higher temperature.

Combination boilers

The combination boiler is basically a continental principle and because of its compactness is making sealed systems more acceptable. However, the aim is only to provide the normal temperature level and not run at higher temperatures and pressures. More details are given in Chapter 10.

Microbore circuits

Small-bore circuits appeared in the 1950s. By the 1970s, it was thought that even small-bore pipes could be made smaller and the idea of microbore became all the rage. It was said that this would be the end of small-bore as small-bore had been the end of the old steel pipes. But microbore is not something radically different from small-bore, it is merely an extension of it.

Table 8.1 shows the load limits of microbore sizes. You can see that as the load becomes smaller than 4000 watts, you can use smaller tube than 15 mm.

To get the maximum possible load through these smaller-diameter tubes, it is necessary to increase the flow rate but, as explained earlier, flow rates in excess of 1 metre per second cause vibration and noise. Microbore tubing is made of a softer copper which can accept a faster flow rate of 1.2 or sometimes 1.5 m/s without causing vibration. The higher flow rates and the greater friction mean pumps with higher heads must be used.

Table 8.1 Load limits of microbore copper tube

Nominal diameter (mm)	Maximum load (watts)	Flow (l/s)
6	750	0.018
8	1500	0.036
10	2500	0.060
12	4100	0.098

Of course, as the heating load increases you move up to 15 mm and 22 mm etc. What the really keen microbore supporters said was that in the average domestic system there is never a radiator with an emission larger than the 15 mm tube load limit of 6058 watts so if each radiator was fed separately you would only need microbore tube. If every radiator was fed directly from the boiler you would end up with a mass of pipes looking like so much spaghetti. It was decided

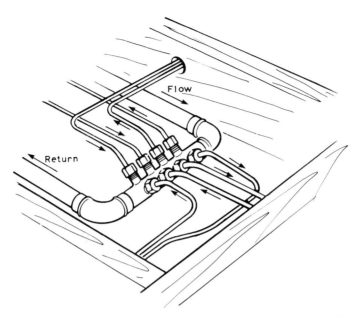

Fig. 8.8. A microbore manifold showing the main flow and return pipes at opposite ends. There is a partition dividing these, and the two pipes serving each radiator must be taken from opposite sides of this partition

that it would be practicable to feed each radiator from a central manifold for each floor. The manifolds would be supplied by a normal two-pipe circuit using small-bore pipes.

Manifolds

When this was all new, there were many weird and wonderful designs of manifolds but the simplest was the Wednesbury 'micrafold'. This type has become the most popular (Fig. 8.8).

Sometimes the manifold method is ideal but quite often it is easier and cheaper to follow normal two-pipe circuitry and reduce to microbore tubing as required.

In spite of its smaller diameter microbore tubing is no cheaper than 15 mm tube. The fittings are as expensive as 15 mm because 15 mm fittings are made in vast quantities. It is important to look carefully at your individual needs if you are thinking about microbore. There are many places where it is a definite advantage but often a simple two-pipe small-bore circuit is cheaper.

9

The chemical effect of water

I have previously referred to the undesirability of pumping water over the open safety vent and of sucking air down it. Two obvious reasons for not wanting this to happen are that, first, the water is supposed to heat the radiators and not the feed and expansion cistern, and secondly circulation might be stopped in various sections by air locks. However, there are other less obvious but equally important reasons for avoiding this.

The reason for having a closed system is to impose a limit to the amount of corrosion that one filling of water can cause. There is no such thing as 'pure water' coming from our taps: it always contains impurities, including those put in by the water board to render all the others harmless. According to the chemical constitution of the water, it is classified as 'hard' or 'soft'.

Hard water

Hard water contains dissolved salts of an alkaline nature and is recognizable by the fact that it is difficult to obtain a lather when using soap as the salts combine with the soap to form a scum. Most hard water has in varying proportions two types of hardness: temporary and permanent. With temporary hardness the salts come out of suspension when heated and are deposited on surfaces with which they are in contact. This effect is most often seen as a scale build-up inside kettles. Once the salts have been deposited, the water will not produce any more scale but a fresh amount of water will deposit another layer. With permanent hardness, the salts are not released by heating and so no scale build-up occurs.

In a closed system, the same water remains in the circuits and after initial deposit of scale, the water is softer and less alkaline than before. If fresh water enters the system the pipework can gradually become blocked by an increasing layer of scale. This is generally caused by the overflow in the feed and expansion cistern being set too low or the initial water level being set too high so that when the water in the system expands into the cistern it overflows and is lost. When the system cools and the level falls, the ball valve will allow more fresh water into the system to replace the quantity lost.

Soft water

The chemical components of soft water give it a slightly acid composition which has a corrosive effect on most metals, particularly when hot and in the presence of oxygen. This causes red and black oxidation of steel known respectively as rust and magnetite. As with hard water, the effect is limited in a closed system.

If soft water is continually entering your system then your heating system is gradually rotting away from the inside. This need not happen to you because I've warned you and because I will explain how to set the overflow in Chapter 14. But there is another, apparently harmless but quite deadly substance in water: air.

Air infiltration

Air is present in water from the tap and is mostly driven out by heating. However, it can be re-absorbed later. When a heating system is first commissioned, the air dissolved in the water is gradually expelled and collects at different high points. During the running-in period it is necessary to go around frequently and vent this air from the high points, which will be fitted with air vents. A favourite place for this is in the radiator closest above the boiler because here the water is hottest and the air released rises to the first high spot.

Of course in a closed system, very little water is in contact with the air and so the air entrapment reduces to virtually nothing. If, however, water is pumped over the vent or air is sucked down the vent, the system water is re-aerated. If all that this caused were continual air locks and the need to vent them, it would be inconvenient and inefficient, but air does more than that. Air contributes to the corrosive properties of the water and, because it contains oxygen, 'recharges' the acid batteries so to speak.

Galvanic action

'Galvanic action' is the name given to the electrical reaction when two dissimilar metals are present in an acid environment. Without this action there would be no car batteries. The degree of action is determined by how dissimilar the metals are in their atomic makeup.

In an electrochemical reaction of this kind one of the metals tends to be eaten away and, using the acid solution as a carrier, is deposited on the other metal. This is similar to electroplating and is not an ideal thing to have occurring all the time in your heating system. As there are copper pipes and steel radiators, there is the potential for this to happen but it will not occur providing that the water is not replaced continually and that air is not allowed to enter the system.

Another effect is the separation of water into its two constituent elements: oxygen and hydrogen. This is called electrolysis and the release of oxygen increases the corrosion and the hydrogen collects at high points. In some systems, venting of radiators has to be carried out regularly and it is usually assumed that it is air collecting but, in some cases, it could be hydrogen. If the vent is opened while a lighted match is held to the escaping 'air' and the flame burns blue, there is hydrogen present and electrolysis is taking place.

Dezincification

Copper and zinc react electrochemically to a greater degree than copper and steel, which is why it is better to use plastic cisterns rather than galvanized. Oddly enough, these two elements mix very well to form brass. Brass is used to make many fittings because, unlike steel, it does not corrode in contact with the air.

The trouble is that in what are known as dezincification areas, the water is particularly suited to the electrolytic action described earlier as similar to electroplating. The zinc part of the brass is the part that gets eaten away and eventually the fittings collapse. This is not a problem in a well-designed heating system, provided the main requirements of no fresh water and no air entry are maintained and so brass fittings can be used on closed central heating systems.

If fittings are used for a direct system or for the secondary side of the domestic hot water system, where water is being continually replaced, then, in a dezincification area, brass must not be used. Special fittings made from alternatives such as gunmetal should be employed. I cannot tell you which are the problem areas because the chemical makeup in different water board areas is not always constant as they may bring in supplies from other areas, which differs from that which they have traditionally supplied. Generally, of course, they are not going to bring in this kind of water where it was not previously supplied but they can do the reverse and a dezincification area will cease to be so. If you use fittings on a direct or hot water open system, first check to see if you live in a dezincification area.

Lead leaching

In certain areas the water may dissolve any lead with which it comes into contact; this is known as leaching and is considered a health hazard. In a closed heating system it is not important but I am mentioning it in case you make any alterations to the tap circuits.

Obviously no one will be using lead pipe but the standard solder-ring fitting contains lead. For tap circuits in these area special fittings are manufactured using a lead-free silver/tin solder and they will be stamped with the BS number 864. They are about 20 per cent dearer than standard fittings.

Cleanliness

Any of the above kinds of damage to a heating system are aggravated if insufficient care is taken to be clean and tidy during installation. If, when cutting tube, copper filings or swarf are allowed to remain in the tube, they will increase chemical reaction and will localize corrosion where they rest. In radiators, the corrosion is first noticed as pinholes and, as the water leaks through and the outside air makes contact with the metal, rust develops rapidly leading to the collapse of the area and the scrapping of the radiator. Swarf and filings can also cause considerable damage to the pump.

When using flux with capillary fittings only the minimum should be applied and care should be taken to ensure that no surplus falls into the tube. Fluxes are corrosive and often of a waxy composition, which makes it difficult to flush them out of the system.

I have seen installers give a radiator a few sharp taps with a hammer to adjust the level, rather than take it off the wall and relocate the brackets: this can cause a stress area in the low-carbon steel, which makes it an easy prey to corrosive attack.

All the materials used in the standard heating system are strong and durable if used correctly and installed cleanly and carefully. A few minutes extra spent taking care at this stage could add years to the life of your system.

Inhibitors

The nasty things which can damage your heating system can be eliminated or greatly reduced by applying certain chemicals to the water in your system. These chemicals are known as inhibitors and different types are available for different boilers and systems. It is a good idea to add one of these to the water soon after starting up the system. However, I must stress that this does not enable you to ignore all the principles of good design or to be careless in installation; it is an extra safeguard, not a substitute for doing the job right in the first place.

10
Selection of hardware

Many aspects of a heating system rely on personal preference but the first thing to decide is the fuel to use and this choice is made for many of us because the obvious first choice, gas, is not available. Where gas is available very few people choose anything else and as this is the most popular fuel I will deal with gas boilers first.

Gas boilers

The old 'town gas' made from coal is now no more and all piped gas supplies are 'natural gas' from the North Sea. When North Sea gas runs out, everything will revert back to a type of town gas again, although it may be made by different processes and research is going ahead on this now.

The advantage of gas is that it needs no storage space, it is instantly controllable, the boilers are cheaper and in addition to all these advantages it is also the cheapest in running costs. However, the government intends to raise the price until it matches other fuels more closely.

There are many types of gas boiler but they fall mainly into three groups: the fire and back-boiler type known as room heaters, the traditional free-standing and the newer wall-mounted.

Room heaters

These are fitted in a fire opening and necesitate taking out the old fire. If a back-boiler was fitted this must also be removed but any copper pipes running from it to the hot water cylinder can often be re-used with the gas boiler.

The hidden boiler provides the central heating and the hot water and at the front there is a clean and controllable fire as a warm focal point in the room. There is a wide range of designs and the fires can have normal radiants with a glowing coal or log effect or even hot ceramic 'coals'.

The flue gases from a gas boiler are acidic and if they condense onto the brickwork of a chimney, discolouration of the inside walls will occur and eventually the chimney will become unsafe and will have to be re-built. This is very expensive but is easily avoided by fitting a stainless steel flue liner, as required by building regulations.

Free-standing

This is the traditional boiler usually seen in the kitchen and there are two types: one has a conventional flue (sometimes called an open flue) rising from it, and the other has a balanced flue.

Fig. 10.1. The Glow worm Co-ordinate LFL. An example of a room heater with a traditional appearance having a log fire effect. Available with a maximum output of 3.6 kW from the fire and 16.4 kW from the back boiler for central heating.

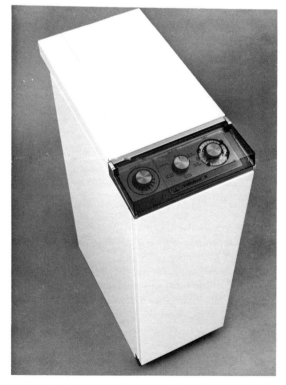

Fig. 10.2. A typical free-standing boiler the Thorn 'M'. Available as here with built-in programmer or with facility for external programmer

Conventional flue. With this type the flue pipe rises from the boiler and may then pass straight up through the house and through the roof. In this case the flue must be a twin-wall type and special distance pieces are necessary to keep it a statutory distance from any combustible parts of the structure.

Another method is for the flue to pass into an existing chimney, and in this case a flue liner must be fitted as with the room heaters; care must be taken to seal around where the flue pipe goes through the brickwork. Alternatively, the flue may pass through an outside wall and continue up the outside of the house. In this case the flue should ideally be twin-walled.

With all conventional flue boilers, the air for combustion must be supplied from the room, and fresh air inlets must be provided for this. The amount of inlet is stated in each boiler installation instructions but a general rule is that the inlet area should be equal to twice the cross-sectional area of the flue. To prevent draughts across the room it is better to place the air inlet near the boiler and not on the opposite side of the room.

In addition to air for combustion, a flow of air is needed to prevent the temperature of the area around the boiler from becoming too high. This is called compartment ventilation and is most important if the boiler is in a restricted space.

Balanced flue. These boilers are more often referred to now as room-sealed because the air for combustion is supplied from outside the room in which the boiler is situated. Although this appliance does not need to take air for combustion from the room, it will still need compartment ventilation.

There are restrictions on where the terminal may be placed; some positions are not suitable for technical reasons (such as close into a corner) because there will be insufficient air flow to supply the boiler or to carry away the flue gases.

Some positions are not allowed by the Building Regulations for safety reasons, such as near opening windows. One further regulation is that a terminal guard must be fitted when the terminal is under 2 m from the ground or any surface to which people may have access; see Fig. 10.3.

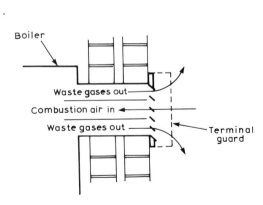

Fig. 10.3. A section through a balanced flue. The terminal guard is only needed if the terminal is below 2 m from any surface on which people may walk

Wall-mounted

Wall-mounted boilers have become very popular recently for the obvious reasons that they take up very little space and can even be fitted into a cupboard. The most popular are room-sealed but open-flue versions can be fitted.

Fig. 10.4. The Glow-worm 'Fuelsaver'. A wall-hung low-water content boiler suitable for normal or sealed systems seen here neatly fitted with kitchen cabinets

Where these boilers are fitted into cupboards the maker's instructions must be followed and the fitting must comply with any local regulations or Building Regulations concerning air supply and proximity to combustible materials. Although a room-sealed model does not require air from the room for combustion, it should be supplied with compartment ventilation to prevent overheating.

Some of these boilers have traditional cast heat exchangers and system design can follow traditional patterns. However, many have low-water-content heat exchangers which need special circuit arrangements covered in Chapter 8.

Combination boilers

These boilers provide heating and hot water, which is heated only as required. The fundamental difference is that the traditional UK principle has been to circulate the boiler water through a coil to heat a store of water, while the continental practice is to circulate cold water from the mains through a coil inside the boiler water.

One type, the Worcester Engineering Heatslave, retains the traditional feed and expansion

Fig. 10.5. The Ideal 'Elan' wall-hung boiler. A new trend in design to match the darker wood-finish kitchen cabinets

Fig. 10.6. The Worcester Engineering 'Heatslave'. This boiler does away with the hot water cylinder, but not the feed and expansion cistern as some continental boilers do. However, this may be preferred to these sealed-system boilers

cistern to provide the static pressure, while another type, such as the Vokera, has an integral sealed system expansion vessel. With both types there is a saving of space and work because no cold water cistern or hot water cylinder is required.

Caution. Because modern wall-hung gas boilers can be fitted in many positions such as inside cupboards, it is often assumed that they can be fitted anywhere. This is not true; they should not be fitted in bedrooms and under no circumstance can any boiler be fitted in a bathroom.

For those living in rural areas without mains gas, there is the alternative of liquid propane gas (LPG). The tank for the fuel is rented from the supply company and the running cost is now, since the fall in oil prices, the most expensive. However, it means that you can have a smaller and quieter boiler and most gas cookers will run off it, which saves on electricity costs.

Oil boilers

Of the two main types, the wallflame is the quieter and, although not absolutely silent, can be fitted indoors. It burns 28 sec oil (kerosene), which is more expensive than the 35 sec (gas oil) used by pressure-jet models.

The traditional pressure jets are too noisy for indoor fitting but some down-firing models are a bit quieter and can be adapted to burn 28 or 35 sec fuel.

Oil-fired boilers may be automatically switched and all forms of control may be used as with gas. However, they are not as convenient as gas, being generally larger and a tank must be provided to store the fuel.

Solid-fuel boilers

Solid-fuel boilers were the first to be used for central heating but lost ground to more automatic fuels. However, with the increase in oil prices they are gaining in popularity, particularly in areas without a gas supply.

Solid-fuel boilers cannot be switched on and off instantly and heating circuit control is normally by switching the pump. Whether the pump is on or off, the fire continues to burn and although the boiler thermostat can reduce the burning rate by operating a damper or a fan, the effect is not immediate.

Fig. 10.7. The Baxi 'Burnall' with underfloor draught. Behind it a back-boiler for hot water and central heating. Dunsley also make more powerful back-boilers to fit behind the Baxi fires in addition to their own combined units

It is therefore important that the hot water cylinder is on a 'gravity' circuit and no valves should be used which could close this circuit. Because of this, the temperature of the cylinder cannot be controlled. As the temperature could be as high as 75°C, this is a point to consider, particularly if there are children in the house. The recommended hot water temperature is 55–60°C. One or even two radiators should also be on 'gravity' and it should not be possible to shut these off either.

Back-boilers

This type ranges from those with an open fire such as the Dunsley Enterprise to closed appliances called room heaters, which are very efficient and can provide full heating in a small house. The existing fire surround must be removed and a fair amount of work is involved. This is not to say it is beyond DIY people but care must be taken and the manufacturer's instructions followed carefully.

Fig. 10.8. A closed solid-fuel room heater, the Parkray 'GL'. Closed room heaters are more efficient than an open fire and back-boiler and can supply larger heating systems

Fig. 10.9. The Trianco 'TRG' free-standing solid-fuel boiler. This is a hopper-fed boiler which generally needs stoking only once a day

Free-standing

Most boilers of this type are now hopper-fed like the Trianco or the Worcester Hoppamat and incorporate a hopper from which 'grains' or 'beans' of anthracite are dropped onto the fire; the combustion rate is determined by a thermostatically-controlled fan. The principle is illustrated diagrammatically in Fig. 10.10. This type does not need very frequent stoking but is expensive.

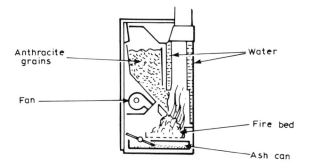

Anthracite grains

Water

Fan

Fire bed

Ash can

Fig. 10.10. A cross-section through a hopper-fed boiler. The anthracite grains, peas or beans are poured into the hopper and they replenish the fire as burning reduces the fuel on the fire bed. The rate of burning is adjusted by a fan controlled by a thermostat

Cookers

Solid-fuel cookers have recently enjoyed a considerable increase in popularity, especially those able to burn different fuels. There are now many more models available, including many new names from the continent. Some cookers provide only hot water in addition to cooking but some are able to supply full central heating. They are very expensive and have the disadvantage of giving out a good deal of heat into the room at all times unless an electric element is fitted to provide cooking facilities in summer. However, the hot water would then have to be heated by electricity also.

Fig. 10.11. An example of the new breed of traditional-looking cookers, The Bosky cooker is able to supply hot water and quite large heating systems. There are two sizes producing respectively around 17 kW and 23 kW. They burn wood and/or solid fuels and the burning rate can be closely controlled. Part of the heat can be diverted from the boiler to the oven as required which really means that the oven can be switched on and off. There is a second slow oven, and in summer or when a quick boost is needed, there is an electric element in the oven to save having to light the fire

Emitters

The choice of emitters is generally dictated by individual preference for the appearance but the different types do have inherent advantages and disadvantages as follows.

Panel radiators

These emitters are relatively inexpensive, they are simple to install and, because of the proportion of radiated heat, they contribute to the overall comfort level as explained in Chapter 1. A disadvantage is that they take up wall space and sometimes make the placing of furniture difficult.

Fig. 10.12. Single and double panel slim-line rolled-top radiators from Thorn. Matching convector rads are also available

Convector radiators

These give a greater emission than panel radiators for the same area because of an increase in convected heat caused by fins welded to the back of single convectors and between doubles. Some manufacturers have gone over completely to convectors but sometimes for appearances, with a small heat requirement, a panel radiator is preferred because the very small convector looks odd. Also, as explained in Chapter 1, the larger the surface area, the more radiant heat is emitted, which improves the comfort level. Because of this, makes such as Barlo and Thorn who supply matching panels and convectors are very popular. These also have rounded tops.

   Some other makes, such as the Stelrad Accord and Dianorm, have seamed tops, which enable attractive top and side panels to be fitted to doubles.

Fig. 10.13. Barlo make a matching range of panel radiators and convectors. Shown here is the rear of a single convector showing the fins which increase the emission

Aluminium radiators

There are some new radiators made from extruded aluminium having no welds and needing no painting, being supplied in a range of colours. Aluminium, in a normal heating system, can present a potentially greater corrosion risk than steel and these radiators need an anti-corrosion treatment and should carry a guarantee of this.

Fig. 10.14. A Dia-norm stove enamelled double convector with top and side grilles, which enhance its appearance

Skirting heating

These units are more expensive but they have some unique properties. They are unobtrusive and provide heat at low level, which assists comfort, although they have very little radiant effect. Because they are fitted around the edges of a room they distribute heat very evenly. They consist of a finned copper tube inside a casing and the emission can be controlled by a damper. Skirting heating reduces the water content of the system and provides a quicker response.

Fig. 10.15. A length of Finrad skirting heating. This make has a veneered wood top and is only 216 mm high and 51 mm deep. It can provide a very even distribution of heat around a room

Fan convectors

These employ a thermostatically controlled fan to increase the air flow over the finned heat exchanger. They are very useful where wall space is limited and Myson produce two models which cannot be equalled in two areas: their overhead convector can be fitted high up and is particularly effective over an outside door which is frequently opened, and the 'kick-space' convector can be fitted neatly into the space under kitchen cabinets.

Because of the electrical connection, fan convectors should not be fitted in bathrooms. They have a low water content and provide a quicker response.

Cylinders

Hot water storage has been covered earlier and the need for an indirect cylinder has been established but I have mentioned only the standard indirect cylinder with a coil heat exchanger.

There is another type called a self-feeding and venting or single feed cylinder; in this the primary water is separated from the secondary by an air lock, which automatically establishes itself when the system is filled. There is no need for a separate feed and expansion cistern. If boiling occurs the heating system is able to vent through this cylinder into the cold water storage cistern. The air lock will re-establish itself afterwards but some mixing of the waters will take place, which is not good for either.

(a)

(b)

(c)

Fig. 10.16. Three types of fan-convector from Myson. (a) The normal wall-hung model may be fitted on any wall and has a large output for the space occupied. (b) The high-level model can be fitted over doorways, or where space is only available high up. (c) The kick-space convector fits neatly into the plinth of most kitchen cabinets and, to save bending, there are remote controls

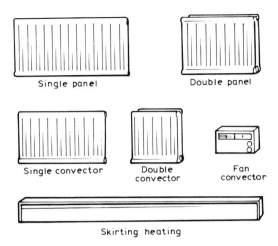

Fig. 10.17. A diagrammatic representation of the space taken up by different types of emitter for the same heat emission

These cylinders are not used very often now because they are more expensive and they cannot be used on large systems, fully pumped systems or with solid-fuel boilers.

Where a direct cylinder is already fitted and the new heating system is to be fully pumped then what is called a conversion element can be fitted into the immersion heater boss. Sometimes a conversion coil can be fitted between the original feed and return tappings.

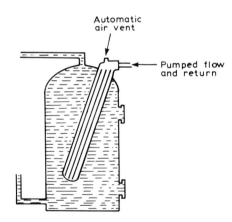

Fig. 10.18. A section through a direct cylinder adapted to indirect operation by inserting a conversion element into the standard electric immersion heater boss

Tube

Tubes are made of different materials, some more suitable than others.

Copper

This is a tried and tested tube; it resists corrosion itself but can contribute to the corrosion of steel radiators if the system is badly designed. It is easy to manipulate, it is available from many manufacturers such as Wednesbury Tube and Yorkshire Metals, a vast range of fittings are available and it will take a fair amount of knocking about in the domestic environment. It is fairly expensive but in real terms is much cheaper than it used to be. It is supplied in 3 m and 6 m lengths.

Stainless steel

This is a safe alternative to copper but is harder and cannot be bent. It looks quite good without paint and cannot conflict with steel radiators to cause corrosion. It comes into its own when copper prices rise as its price does not fluctuate as much.

Black steel

This is very much cheaper than copper and stainless steel but must be threaded to take fittings and is not really suited for domestic systems. Even in industrial work it is used now only in the larger sizes.

Coated mild steel

This tube should not be used. Although it is very cheap and can be used with ordinary fittings and, in theory, can be used without corrosion, in practice it has proved to be short-lived and many systems have had to be completely re-fitted.

Nylon

This is not a generally approved material although it is sometimes used with microbore systems. I would not recommend it.

CPVC tube

This is a new material for hot water applications and is now approved under certain conditions. It is cheaper than the metal tubes and the joints are made using a solvent which effectively welds the material. I have found it easy to make the joints without any leaking but I would prefer a bit longer testing.

Fittings

Apart from the solvent-weld type used with CPVC tube, there are two basic choices: a blowlamp and solder, or a spanner or wrench.

Compression

These fittings are made of brass or gun metal and are tightened on to the tube. The procedure is described in Chapter 14.

Capillary

These fittings rely on a solder infill to make the seal and are very strong when made. The easiest type for the newcomer is the solder-ring type; this has the solder built-in. The end-feed type must have a solder strip applied when hot and requires a little more skill.

The disadvantages of capillary fittings are that, once made, you cannot change your mind very easily; and they cannot be used throughout because some joints must have the manouverability of compression fittings.

Iron

There are parts of the system where you might need iron fittings such as bushes to reduce tappings as required. These are not used much in domestic surroundings as they used to be, although oil tank fittings are all in iron.

Ancillary items

The other items in a system such as cisterns, pumps and valves are straightforward and there are no important distinctions to be made between one type and another. However, the choice of controls needs a chapter to itself.

11
Controls

In Chapter 1, I discussed comfort, and pointed out that the human body, in a comfortable environment, loses heat at an average rate of 100 watts. It is only when this rate varies too much that we are uncomfortable, and the obvious way of controlling our heat loss is to provide a surrounding temperature at which we are comfortable.

Just providing heat is obviously not enough; the essential thing is to provide stable temperatures, which means that some form of continuous monitoring of our surroundings must be arranged. As control of temperature is the prime consideration, this is the first area to look at.

Temperature

The first heating medium was the open fire and the basic control was to build large fires on very cold days and smaller fires on less cold days. All control methods from manual to electronic have two components: the first senses the temperature and the second adjusts the heat output. With the open fire, during each day a finer control was obtained by the occupant 'sensing' temperature and then 'adjusting' the burning rate by increasing or reducing the air supply for combustion.

The first central-heating systems were based on solid-fuel boilers and the boiler output was controlled in much the same way as the open fire by adjusting stoking rate and air supply. If this had been all the control available, it would have been a bad deal because at least with the fire you did not have to leave your living room to adjust the output.

However, emission into each room was by radiator and the water supply to each one could be adjusted by a hand-control radiator valve. The sensing mechanism was still the body and the adjustment was manual. On the other side of each radiator there should be another valve called the lockshield valve; I will deal with this in the next chapter because it isn't part of the control system but is related to the sizing of the pipes and radiators.

Pumps

When pumps were introduced it was possible, by switching on and off, to control the flow of water to the entire heating circuit. The simplest way was to have a switch for the occupant to operate but this would still be human sensing and adjustment.

It would be more convenient to have a device which could automatically sense the temperature and switch the pump on and off as required and the first automatic control of temperature, the room thermostat, began to appear in heating installations.

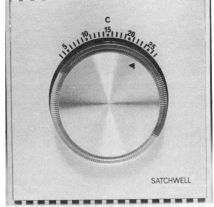

Fig. 11.1. A typical radiator hand-control valve   Fig. 11.2. A room thermostat by Satchwell

Room thermostat

The room thermostat is convenient because it saves people having to adjust everything manually. However, it is not as good at sensing human comfort as the human body because, as explained in Chapter 1, it senses only air temperature and itself needs adjusting, as the radiant heat varies.

The radiators for each room must be sized accurately so that all the rooms reach their temperatures at the same time because the single room thermostat switches them all off together. However, even with the most careful sizing, other influences upset the balance: cooking in the kitchen or a disco in the living room will raise the temperature of those rooms faster than the others.

The thermostat must therefore be placed in a representative position for the whole house so that it is unlikely to receive extra heat gains and switch off the heating when all the other rooms are still not up to temperature. The hall is a favourite position because it is the one room which will not be overheated by other influences. However, it is affected in the opposite way by cold air from the door opening and this position is often criticized because of this. As the cold air does represent a genuine heat requirement and will have to be heated somewhere and as no other position appears any better, I think generally it is as good a place as any for a single thermostat.

Of course, the thermostat should not be in a direct draught or over a radiator or in direct sunlight. It can give reasonable control but you can see it is not perfect; on the other hand it is inexpensive.

Thermostatic radiator valves

It would help, from a sensing point of view, if each room had its own room thermostat but it would make no difference to the adjustment because the pump would still affect the whole system.

The answer to more individual room control is the thermostatic radiator valve. This has a non-electric sensor operating a valve fitted instead of the hand control valve. There are two types: one has the sensor built-in, and the other has a remote sensor which is supposed to be more accurate, the argument being that the built-in sensor is affected by heat from the pipework below it.

As the valve can be set at different sensing levels, it can be set to allow for this local heating. When you think of the ease of fitting a valve with a built-in sensor, the extra cost of the remote model and the fact that both sense only air temperature, the built-in model seems a better bargain.

It is possible for all thermostatic valves to be closed at a particular time and, as they are non-electric and cannot be wired back to switch off the pump, a bypass must be provided so that circulation is not stopped suddenly.

Thermostatic valves on every radiator may seem expensive but they can save a lot of fuel.

Fig. 11.3. The Drayton thermostatic radiator valve. This is the integral sensor model but remote sensor models are available

Fig. 11.4. A Drayton Cyltrol valve for non-electric control of hot water

Boiler thermostat

On the early solid-fuel systems the hot water was on 'gravity' circulation and the cylinder was needed to dissipate excess heat from the boiler because solid fuel cannot be turned off. This meant that the hot water at the taps was at boiler temperature with a risk of scalding. When gas and oil boilers were introduced, it was possible to fit a thermostat to the boiler so that when it reached the set temperature, the burners were switched off. Now the cylinder was not needed as a heat-leak and its temperature could be controlled.

One cannot switch off solid fuel but more modern solid-fuel boilers have some form of thermostatic control. The thermostat adjusts either a damper or a fan to control the air supply or, with a hopper-fed boiler, the rate at which fuel is fed in.

Cylinder thermostat

Until recently the circulation to the cylinder continued to be by 'gravity', and to control the flow it was not necessary to switch anything on or off electrically; it could be controlled by any device which could open and close a valve in response to temperature changes. The Drayton Cyltrol is a popular non-electric thermostatic valve for this purpose. The valve is placed in the return to the boiler and senses that temperature. A more recent version, the Tapstat, is placed in the same position but it senses the temperature at a position on the cylinder itself by a remote sensor. The argument here is the same as for a remote sensor thermostatic radiator valve.

The purpose of control is to provide comfort with economy. Some form of thermostatic control will do this while the room is occupied but there is no need for the heating to be on at all when unoccupied for any length of time, and for this we need time controls.

Time control

Time-switches

The basic time control is manual: you switch the boiler on when you want it, and off when you don't. However, as most wet systems have a fairly slow response, we must wait for the system to get up to temperature. How much better to get the warm-up period over before you enter the room. For this a time-switch (often incorrectly called a time clock) is fitted.

Fig. 11.5. A time-switch by Smiths, the Centroller 30

This device makes it possible to set the times of operation each day. A common pattern for years has been two 'on' and two 'off' periods per day, but now there are electronic switches which can provide far more variations than this. There are also means of omitting certain days from the normal pattern.

Programmers

With combined heating and hot water systems, we may want hot water when the heating is off, particularly in summer. For this a special switch called a programmer is used: if hot water is needed, the boiler is switched on; if heating is needed, both the boiler and pump are switched on.

If heating only is required the boiler must be on and, as the hot water is on 'gravity', the cylinder will also be heated. This doesn't worry many people because generally a store of hot water is always needed and once up to temperature, the 'gravity' circulation stops anyway. However, it does not allow completely independent time control of the two circuits.

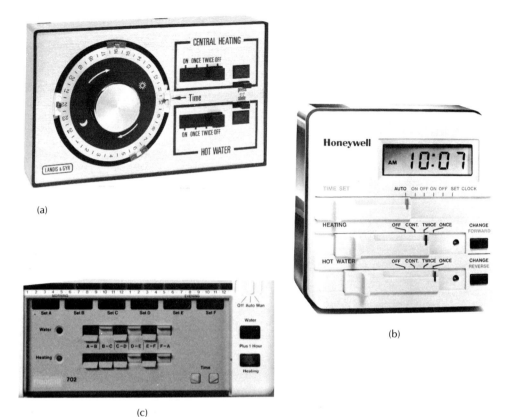

(a)

(b)

(c)

Fig. 11.6. (a) A Landis and Gyr programmer with traditional electric clock with two 'on' and two 'off' periods for separate time control of heating and hot water. (b) A Honeywell programme using solid-state electronic timing but with the established pattern of two 'on' and two 'off' periods. (c) A Randall programmer using electronic control to give a number of variations in the timing pattern

Fig. 11.7. A Satchwell two-port zone valve for separate control of circuits

Zone controls

It is not only the heating and hot water circuits which may want independent control. If you think about it, you are unlikely to want the bedrooms heated to full temperature during the day, or the living room in the morning when you are getting up to go to work. In view of this, it is surprising how few homes have any separation of the heating into different timed areas.

A zone valve may be controlled by a room thermostat, but it is more commonly operated by a time switch. For a family which is out all day, one zone might come on in the morning comprising the bedrooms and bathroom, and another in the late afternoon for the living room, dining room and kitchen. The bedrooms and bathroom circuit could switch on just before bedtime and go off an hour or so later. A typical circuit arrangement is shown in Fig. 11.8.

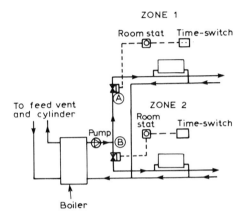

Fig. 11.8. Separate control of two heating zones by two two-port valves. Valve A adjusts the flow to zone 1 and valve B to zone 2. Each is controlled by a room thermostat and time-switch

Boiler switching

With many controls until the late 1970s, the wiring was independent of the boiler. In the simplest, a room thermostat switched the pump on and off. When circulation stopped, the stationary water in the boiler was rapidly heated and the boiler thermostat switched the burners off.

The hot water circulation might be stopped by a non-electric valve and again the boiler was switched off by the boiler thermostat and when zone valves were used, the same boiler thermostat was relied on to control boiler operation.

The trouble with this was that when the water in the boiler cooled, the boiler thermostat would turn on the fuel supply, whether any circuits needed heat or not. This was known as cycling and is not good for the boiler or the burners. To avoid this, modern controls link into the boiler circuit so that when, for example, a zone valve receives a signal from a thermostat to close, another signal is sent to the boiler to switch off. Of course it stays on for as long as any one circuit is calling for heat.

Fully pumped systems

These circuits have been described earlier and the main difference from a control aspect is that as both heating and hot water circulation is by the same pump, there can be no independent

Fig. 11.9. A Satchwell cylinder stat shown attached to a foam-insulated cylinder; the foam has been cut away so that the thermostat can sense the temperature

control by switching the pump. The need is exactly the same as with two heating zones, and two zone valves are used.

The temperature of the heating circuit is sensed by a room thermostat which adjusts the heating circuit zone valve. The cylinder temperature is sensed by a cylinder thermostat which adjusts the cylinder zone valve. For this we need an electric thermostat which is usually strapped to the cylinder and wired to the zone valve.

With a fully pumped system, radiators may be fitted with thermostatic valves, which means that the heating circuit does not need a zone valve controlled by a room thermostat. However, whether there is a room thermostat or individual thermostatic valves, there is likely to be some need for time control.

Diverter valves

The need for hot water and heating does not necessarily occur at the same time and, in a fully pumped system, it is possible to fit a single valve as in Fig. 11.11, instead of two zone valves, to divert the flow to whichever circuit needs it. It is possible to give priority to one circuit or the other, usually the hot water circuit. As all the boiler power is going into the cylinder and not just that part of the output allocated to the hot water need, it will take a very short time to warm up, maybe only 45 minutes or so.

If the system is timed to come on before you awake or before you return home, this 45 minutes can be allowed for and the hot water and heating can be up to temperature for when you arrive. The only problem is that, if the cylinder is emptied, the heating circuit receives no heat until the cylinder is up to temperature again and on a cold day this might not be acceptable. Because of this, the most popular diverter systems now allow for a sharing of the flow if both circuits need heat.

Fig. 11.10. Honeywell diverter three-port valve for priority sharing

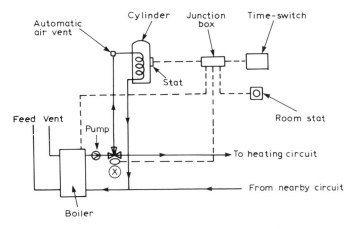

Fig. 11.11. Fully pumped system incorporating three-port diverter valve at X

Optimizers

An optimizer is supposed to sense the outdoor temperatures and adjust various valves to overcome the problems of delay between outdoor changing conditions and the usual internal sensing devices. To do this properly, a thorough understanding of the principles of building response (as described briefly in Chapter 2) is needed, and a means of allowing for the variations in individual properties.

Many expensive and doubtful boxes are being sold which are nothing more than time switches with odd electronic bits, and which have very little to commend them. They are sold by salesmen who give the impression of knowing a great deal about heating and use lots of phrases like 'modern technology' and 'solid-state electronics'. Large savings are claimed in fuel costs, which can be made equally by other makes supplied through the normal channels, and there are plenty to choose from.

Ancillary controls

There are one or two controls which are not directly involved with the comfort requirements of time and temperature but which deal with the occasional problem.

Frost stat

When a house is left unattended in winter, it is wasteful to leave the heating system on permanently, but if it is off all the time water could freeze in the pipes resulting in enormous damage. A frost stat is a thermostat for low temperatures which is fitted near the most vulnerable part of the system. If the boiler is in an outside boiler house then that is likely to be the spot or if there are pipes passing through particularly cold areas, that will be it.

The frost-stat should be set to a few degrees above freezing and positioned where it will be affected moderately by the warmth from the part of the circuit it is protecting. If this is not done you might as well leave the heating on full because, at low temperatures, the frost stat will switch the system on and if it does not receive some of the heat it will continue to keep the boiler running until the ambient temperature improves.

Check valve

Sometimes, particularly in systems which have the pump in the return, circulation will continue by 'gravity' in the heating circuit with the pump off. As this makes it impossible to control the heating properly a check valve can be fitted. This has a weight in it which can be moved by pump pressure but not by weaker natural convection currents.

12
The design of a heating system

The theoretical principles behind heating design have all been covered earlier so in this chapter we can get straight down to the measurements and the working out.

Temperatures

The recommended temperatures, from BS 5449, are shown in Table 12.1 but the final choice is up to you. To calculate the heat losses, the U-value for each part of the structure must be found; this is then multiplied by the area and then by the temperature difference. This can apply to internal walls as well as external.

If one room is at, say 21°C and an adjacent room is at 18°C then, when we come to calculate the heat losses for each room, we must calculate the losses from the first room and the gain into the next. This is an extra chore but it does not affect the overall heat loss from the house; it merely ensures that each room gets its correct assessment. One way of avoiding the extra work is to design all rooms to the same temperature, which is becoming a more common practice now, particularly if thermostatic radiator valves are fitted. The valves can then be adjusted to give temperatures according to the changing uses to which the room may be put.

Table 12.1 Temperature and air changes

	Temperature °C	Air changes per hour
Living room	21	1.0
Dining room	21	2.0
Bedrooms	18	0.5
Hall and landing	16	1.5
Bathroom	22	2.0
Kitchen	18	2.0
WC	18	1.5

Outside design temperature −1°C.

Heat-loss calculations

To demonstrate the method of designing a system, it is best to work to an example. The floor plans shown in Fig. 12.1 are of an actual design taken from my files, which is a useful exercise because it takes into account alterations resulting in three different types of outside wall.

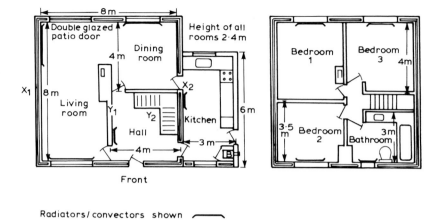

Radiators/convectors shown

Fig. 12.1. Floor plans of house construction as follows:

Walls. Main house outside: brick; cavity; brick; plaster. Kitchen front: brick; cavity; lightweight block; plaster. Kitchen others: 220 mm solid brick; plaster. Downstairs internal: plaster, 220 mm solid brick; plaster. Upstairs internal: plaster; medium-weight block; plaster.

Roofs. Kitchen: Three layers felt and asphalt; 20 mm tongued and grooved air space; 75 mm glass fibre; plasterboard. Main roof: 10 mm tiles on battens; felt; air space; 75 mm glass fibre; plasterboard.

Floors. Ground: solid concrete and screed uninsulated. Intermediate: 20 mm tongued and grooved boards; air space; plasterboard.

Window areas. Living room: 2.5m^2 single glazed; 5m^2 double glazed. Dining room: 2.5m^2 single glazed. Kitchen: 4m^2 single glazed. Bedroom 1: 2m^2 single glazed. Bedroom 2: 2m^2 single glazed. Bedroom 3: 2m^2 single glazed. Bathroom: 1m^2 single glazed.

The property was originally built with a solid wall garage, but a previous owner had converted the garage into a kitchen, the original kitchen into a dining room, and the lounge-dining room into a through living room.

Both leaves of the original cavity wall are of brick but the new cavity wall at the front of the kitchen has a lightweight block inner leaf. The other walls of the kitchen remain as the old solid construction.

Walls and roof

Heat transfer and U-values were explained in earlier chapters; a list of the most common U-values is given in Table 12.2 and generally you need only refer to this. However, it is impossible to cover all possibilities and if you have a different structure you can look back to thermal transmittance in Chapter 4 and work out your own U-value for almost anything.

For example, the roof values in the table do not allow for 75 mm insulation; you could interpolate between the 50 mm and 100 mm values but I have shown the resistance calculation in Table 12.3 to demonstrate the method.

Floor

When discussing floors in Chapter 4, I said it was probably not worthwhile taking the floor of each room separately, particularly with a high degree of connection, which an open-plan house like this certainly has, and we did not do it in this actual case. However, just for fun and to

Table 12.2 Most commonly-occurring U-values

	Amount of insulation		
	None	25 mm	50 mm
External cavity walls (plastered inside)			
Brick–cavity–brick	1.41	0.75	0.56
Brick–cavity–lightweight block	0.95	0.58	0.47
External cavity walls (rendered outside, plastered inside)			
Concrete/brick–cavity–brick	1.35	0.73	0.55
Concrete/brick–cavity–lightweight block	0.90	0.57	0.46
Other external cavity walls			
Tile-clad–cavity–plasterboard	2.27	0.94	0.66
Timberclad–cavity–plasterboard	1.75	0.83	0.61
Solid external walls (plastered inside)			
105 mm brick	2.94	1.03	0.71
220 mm brick	2.13	0.86	0.56
335 mm brick	1.64	0.82	0.54
300 mm stone	2.22	0.93	0.59
450 mm stone	1.75	0.84	0.55
Internal walls			
105 mm plaster–brick–plaster	2.12	N/A	N/A
220 mm plaster–brick–plaster	1.53	N/A	N/A
Plaster–lightweight block–plaster	1.20	N/A	N/A
Plasterboard–studding–plasterboard	1.85	N/A	N/A
Pitched roofs	*None*	*50 mm*	*100 mm*
Tiles on battens–loft space–plasterboard	2.77	0.64	0.35
Tiles on battens on felt–space–plasterboard	2.08	0.62	0.34
Flat roofs			
Chippings–asphalt–chipboard–space–plasterboard	1.45	0.55	0.33
Doors			
Internal: can be taken as U-value of wall in which situated			
External: glazed — same as window U-value			
solid	1.96		
Windows (including frame)	*Single glazed*	*Double glazed*	
Metal frames	5.60	3.10	
Wood frames	4.20	2.50	
Intermediate floors	*Heat flow up*	*Heat flow down*	
Plasterboard–air space–tongued and grooved boards	1.45	1.30	

Table 12.3 Calculation of roof U-value

Component	Resistance (m² °C/W)
Roof outside boundary layer	0.04
Tiles (20 mm × 0.0012)	0.02
Loft space	0.18
Insulation (75 mm × 0.025)	1.89
Ceiling (12 mm × 0.063)	0.07
Inside boundary air layer	0.10
Total resistance	2.30

U-value = 1/2.30 = 0.43 W/m² °C

demonstrate it, suppose we divide the floor into three areas: the kitchen (6 m × 3 m) with three edges exposed, the living room (8 m × 4 m) with three exposed edges and the dining room and hall together (8 m × 4 m) which we can take as two edges.

Let us look at a similar-sized room. 5 m × 7.5 m in Table 4.3 (Chapter 4) is the nearest size to the living room 8 m × 4 m and gives a U-value of 0.89 W/m^2 °C. As 8 m × 4 m is slightly smaller in area, which increases the U-value, I would take it as 0.9 W/m^2 °C.

If you decide not to bother with individual areas, the nearest size to the whole house floor area in Table 4.3 is 10 m × 7.5 m for which the U-value is 0.70 W/m^2 °C. The U-values applicable to this building are shown in Table 12.4.

Table 12.4 Sample-house U-values

	U-value (W/m^2 °C)
Structure	
Main cavity wall	1.41
Kitchen front wall	0.95
Kitchen rear and side walls	2.13
Wall between kitchen and house	1.19
Internal walls, upstairs	2.22
Internal walls, downstairs	1.53
Intermediate floor	
Heat flow up	1.45
Heat flow down	1.30
Kitchen flat roof	0.42
Main roof	0.43
Single glazed windows	5.60
Double glazed patio doors	3.10

Floors	U-value (four edges)		Factor	Adjusted U-value
Living room	0.90	×	0.8 =	0.72
Dining room/hall	0.90	×	0.6 =	0.54
Kitchen	1.12	×	0.8 =	0.90
Overall (average)	0.70			0.70

Air changes

The recommended air changes to use are shown in Table 12.1. If there are particularly ill-fitting windows or doors then higher rates could be used. However, I think it would be more sensible to improve draught-proofing and use the rates in the table.

Table 12.5 Heat loss from living room at 21°C

Surface	Area (m^2)	U-value (W/m^2 °C)		Temperature difference (°C)		Loss (W)	Gain (W)
Floor	32.0	0.72	×	22	=	507	—
Side wall	19.2	1.41	×	22	=	596	—
Rear wall	4.6	1.41	×	22	=	143	—
Front wall	7.1	1.41	×	22	=	220	—
Loss to hall	8.4	1.53	×	5	=	64	—
Ceiling	32.0	1.45	×	3	=	139	—
Rear window	5.0	3.10	×	22	=	341	—
Front window	2.5	5.60	×	22	=	308	—
Air change	76.8 m^3 × 0.33 × 1.5 × 22				=	836	—
Total heat loss from room						3154	—

Table 12.6 Heat loss from bedroom 1 at 18°C

Surface	Area (m²)	U-value (W/m² °C)		Temperature difference (°C)		Loss (W)	Gain (W)
Floor	18.0	1.45	×	3	=		78
Side wall	10.8	1.41	×	19	=	289	
Front wall	7.6	1.41	×	19	=	204	
To landing	2.0	2.20	×	2	=	9	
Ceiling/roof	18.0	0.43	×	19	=	147	
Window	2.0	5.60	×	19	=	213	
Air change	43.2 m³ × 0.33 × 0.5 × 19				=	135	
Total heat loss from room						997	78
						−78	
						919	

Working to the BS 5449 recommended air changes puts the dining room at 2 and the living room at 1 air change. Here the dining room and living room are effectively one space and it would be pointless to calculate for different temperatures and air changes so I will use a compromise value of $1\frac{1}{2}$ changes.

I have worked out the losses for the living room and bedroom 1 in detail (Tables 12.5 and 12.6). Note that there is a gain of 78 watts from the living room into bedroom 1; the remainder of the 139 watts lost through the ceiling of the living room will be a gain into bedroom 2. As practice you might like to calculate one or two of the other rooms and see if you get to the individual room losses I have listed.

Sizing emitters

Whether you choose radiators, skirting heating, fan convectors or a mixture, the heat emission will depend on the difference in temperature between the mean water temperature and the room temperature. Until 1983 it was enough to know that the emission figures given by all manu-facturers was based on the traditional temperature difference between water at 170°F and room at 70°F, which translated into metric became a water temperature of 76.67°C and air tempera-ture of 21.11°C.

In 1983 radiators were first kitemarked to BS 3528 on a proper metric basis to do away with the odd fractions caused by converting from Fahrenheit to Centigrade. The mean water temperature is now 80°C with a room temperature of 20°C giving a difference of 60°C. However, other types of emitter may not give figures based on this new standard and you should check to see on what temperature difference the figures are based.

In the good old days, if your room temperature was to be 21.11°C (the old 70°F), you just took the output on the manufacturer's leaflet when selecting your radiator. If you planned a different temperature, then you applied a simple correction factor.

We now have a peculiar situation in that the standard has changed for radiators but not for boilers. In order to obtain the standard emission at a room temperature of 20°C the water must be at 80°C but British boilers are designed to provide a mean temperature of 76.67°C. This means that the emissions, shown for a room temperature of 20°C in the leaflets, may not be obtainable and a slightly larger radiator may be needed.

No doubt there are thoughts about bringing boilers into line. If there is any purpose in having standards, this should have been done at the same time as radiators or before; it may be that over the years boiler manufacturers will raise the working temperature to make the achieving of the stated radiator emissions, at the stated room temperature, a possibility and not something as mis-leading as at present.

The mean temperature referred to is that between the flow and return boiler temperatures. To provide a mean of 80°C on the standard 10°C drop around the circuit, the flow must be 85°C and the return 75°C. If the boiler can only give a flow temperature of 82°C as most can, then in order to obtain a mean of 80°C, the return must be at 78°C, which is a drop of only 4°C and quite out of the question as it would need a much larger volume of water, which would be too much for small-bore pipes.

To reduce the confusion a little until the 'standards' are standardized, use Table 12.7 according to the flow temperature of the boiler.

Table 12.7 Radiator sizing factors

Room temperature (°C)	Boiler flow temperature 82.2°C	85.0°C
25	1.21	1.12
24	1.18	1.09
23	1.15	1.07
22	1.12	1.04
21	1.10	1.02
20	1.07	1.00
19	1.05	0.98
18	1.03	0.96
17	1.01	0.94
16	0.99	0.92
15	0.97	0.91

To find radiator emission to look for in list, multiply heat loss by factor.
To find actual emission of radiator, divide rated emission in list by factor.

Whatever factor is used, if there is no radiator exactly to suit then the next size up should be taken. Obviously you must use your judgment here; if the nearest one is only 10 watts short, it would be unnecessarily expensive to jump up say, 400, watts to the next size; the 10 watts short would not make any noticeable difference. As a rough guide, 5 per cent of the required emission will make 1°C difference in temperature achieved and then only when the outside temperature is at the design level of −1°C.

The actual choice of radiator depends not only on the emission but also on the space available. In this example a radiator was required in the kitchen to provide heat centrally but the minimum of wall space was to be used. A possible choice might have been a 'kick-space' fan convector but some radiant surface was asked for. The best compromise was a double convector.

In some long rooms, such as the living room here, it may be possible to obtain the emission required with one radiator, but it is often better to fit two or more to provide the heat more evenly. This is even more necessary when there are large areas of glass, which can cause cold spots. As I showed in Chapter 1, even double glazing needs a radiator to compensate for its cooling effect. The selected emitters are listed in Table 12.8.

Pipe runs

When the radiators have been chosen and marked in position on your plan, you can mark the route the pipes must take. A number of factors affect the placing of pipes. They need to be as short as possible but the shortest route may not be practicable. Ideally they should be hidden but this may be impossible in some places.

In our real-life example, the lady of the house wanted the boiler away from the working area in the position shown. Because of the flat roof, the pipes had to rise from the boiler and run across

Table 12.8 Radiator selection

Room	Temperature (°C)	Heat loss (watts)	Factor	Radiator emission to look for	Selected radiator	Rated emission
Living room	(21)	1577	1.10	1735	520×2450 SP	1731
Dining room	(21)	1445	1.10	1590	620×1850 SP	1549
Kitchen	(18)	2313	1.03	2382	720×1200 DC	2394
Hall Landing	(16)	436	0.99	432	620×500 SP	439
Bedroom 1	(18)	919	1.03	957	520×1300 SP	943
Bedroom 2	(18)	756	1.03	779	520×1100 SP	803
Bedroom 3	(18)	898	1.03	925	520×1300 SP	943
Bathroom	(22)	1473	1.12	1650	720×1300 SC	1653

The living-room loss of 3154W has been split into two requirements of 1577W to provide more even heat from two radiators. Because of limited space on the landing, the hall radiator is sized to allow for the landing loss also. Some selected radiator emissions are slightly below the requirement but by such a small amount as to have no effect. The alternative is to move up to a much-too-large radiator.

at ceiling level before entering the house; they were boxed in neatly and papered over so that no-one would notice without being told. The only way of hiding them completely would have been to pull down part of the ceiling and re-plaster.

In this particular case, when we looked at the plans, we could see that with this layout, there must be a steel joist somewhere. We asked the client to check, and in fact there were two: one running between x_1 and x_2 and the other between y_1 and y_2. Because of this, pipes had to enter the house from the kitchen at two points and the steel joists made it impossible to run a micro-bore system from a central manifold, which was the original request.

When planning pipe runs which run across joists, remember to keep the pipes near walls. Notches have to be cut to take the pipes and they have a more weakening effect in the centre of the joist; of course they should not be cut any deeper than is necessary. In countless books on this subject, I have read that the joist is stronger if holes are drilled for the pipes, and that notches should not be cut.

One has only to install one system to know this is virtually impossible, which gives some idea of the practical experience of the writers concerned. The only way it could be done would be to have all your pipe cut into 400 mm lengths to fit in between the joists, push each length through the hole and connect to the next one, using an extra 50 mm length to make up for the joist width, and a coupler.

In connection with pipe fitting, you will often hear joist direction mentioned, but this has no bearing on pipe runs. If you have radiators where you want, then the pipes have to get to them. Look at your own house; see the layout of the joists and decide: can you design a system so that the pipes always run between the joists?

Solid floors

Where there are suspended wood floors downstairs, the pipes can run underneath but if the floors are solid, as in our example, there are different ways of tackling the problem.

You can run pipes around the skirting, which looks ugly, and means going up and over every doorway. You can cut channels in the floor, which risks breaking the damp-proof membrane and is hard work. Arrangements must also be made to cover the channels because you cannot just fill them in to match the screed. The best way in my experience is to drop pipes down from the upstairs circuit in a corner near the downstairs radiator and neatly box-in the pipes afterwards.

Pipe sizing

The limitations of different pipe sizes were discussed in Chapter 6 and the pipes are sized according to Table 12.9. The limits are for the room heating requirement, not the emission that the radiator is capable of.

Table 12.9 Load limits and heat emission of copper tube

Nominal diameter (mm)	Maximum load (watts)	Emission (W/m)* Insulated	Emission (W/m)* Uninsulated
6	750	6	20
8	1500	8	26
10	2500	10	31
12	4100	11	37
15	6000	14	47
22	13400	19	64
28	22500	24	80
35	35000	28	95

*Emission when pipes in unheated space at −1°C.

At this stage it helps to draw a rough isometric layout of the system similar to that in Fig. 12.2, marking each room's heating requirement and putting a letter alongside each section of pipework. As you determine the pipe sizes, they can also be marked.

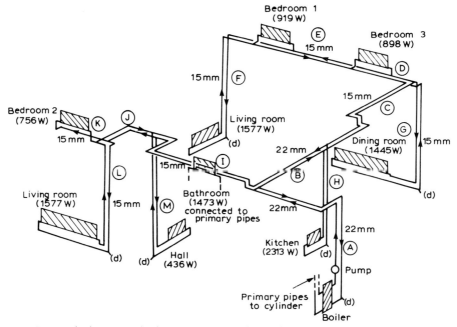

Fig. 12.2. Between bedroom 1 and 3 the pipes must carry the combined load of the living room 1577W and the 919W of bedroom 1, which is 2496W and easily within 15 mm capacity — we could use 10 mm tube if we wished. Section C is carrying the total load of the living room (1577W), bedroom 1 (919W), bedroom 3 (898W) and the dining room (1445W), which comes to 4839W and still 15 mm tube is sufficient. The kitchen radiator is itself supplied by 15 mm tube but its addition to the circuit means that the pipes in section B carry 7152W. Since this is too much for 15 mm tube, 22 mm will be used here. Along section A the pipes are carrying the full load of all radiators totalling 9921W, excluding the bathroom, and 22 mm tubes is used here. At all drops (d) a drain must be fitted

Pipe losses

The emission from pipework is small in relation to the radiators and whatever heat any exposed pipework may emit into a room, it relieves the radiators of providing. The load on the circuit remains the same and is the heat requirement of the areas being served by the circuit.

If pipes enter into unheated areas, such as under a downstairs suspended wood floor or in an unheated garage, the emissions must be allowed for in pipe sizing because it is an additional load on the boiler; it must provide that heat as well as the heating requirements of the house. The pipe emissions are listed in Table 12.9.

Domestic hot water

As explained previously, the hot water is provided by an indirect cylinder. As the water feeding the taps, in the secondary circuit, is separate from the heating water, a separate storage cistern is needed.

Power for hot water

To raise the temperature of cold water to around 60°C in one hour, a power input of 65 watts is required for each litre. A cylinder to BS 1566 of 117 litres capacity would need 7605 W (65 W × 117) maintained for one hour.

If three hours are allowed, only one third of the one-hour rate will be needed, which is 2535 W. The quicker the cylinder is heated and the larger the volume, the more power is needed from the boiler. Generally the re-heat time allowed is three hours. This is satisfactory for most households but a large family might need a quicker recovery time or a larger-volume cylinder and the different allowances are shown in Table 12.10.

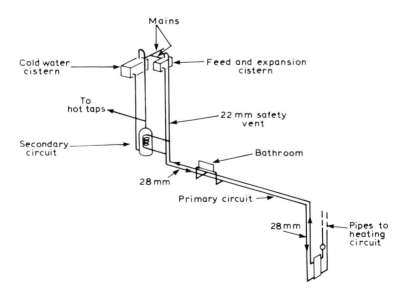

Fig. 12.3. The 'gravity' hot water circuit including the bathroom radiator. From the cylinder to the feed and expansion cistern, the minimum size pipe for the feed and the vent is 22 mm

Table 12.10 Cylinder heat allowances

| Capacity | | Re-heat periods | |
	1 hr	2 hr	3 hr
117 litre	7605W	3802W	2535W
140 litre	9100W	4550W	3033W

If the cylinder is on a fully pumped circuit, which was explained in Chapter 8, the pipes are sized as for a radiator of the appropriate loading, i.e. for a 117-litre three-hour re-heat needing 7605 watts, 22 mm pipe would be used according to Table 12.9. If the cylinder is on a 'gravity' circuit, then the pipes must be sized according to Table 12.11. It is not practicable to go for a shorter reheat period than three hours with 'gravity' circulation because the pipes needed may become too large.

Table 12.11 Primary pipe sizes (mm) three-hour reheat period

| Height from boiler centre to cylinder centre (m) | Cylinder capacity (litres) | | | | | | | |
	117	140	117	140	117	140	117	140
0.5	28	35	35	35	35	35	35	42
1.0	28	28	28	28	28	35	35	35
1.5	28	28	28	28	28	28	28	28
2.0	28	28	28	28	28	28	28	28
Horizontal distance boiler to cylinder (m):	4		6		8		10	

With solid-fuel boilers, the cylinder must be on a 'gravity' circuit and also at least one radiator to dissipate excess heat. In this particular installation the client preferred a 'gravity' circuit to the cylinder and, although it was a gas boiler and a 'gravity'-fed radiator is not necessary, he wanted the bathroom put on the cylinder circuit so that it could be warmed and towels dried, when the central heating was off.

Some people still ask for a radiator on the hot water circuit with fully pumped systems but when this is done, the cylinder is heated very quickly and the radiator is not on long enough to be worthwhile.

Pump sizing

Sizing the pump used to be a long process when only fixed-head pumps were available but now that all domestic pumps have variable heads, all that is needed is to order a pump according to the size of your heating system in watts.

If you need to size the pump because of some unusual situation then two figures must be established:

1. The water flow rate
2. The frictional head loss of the circuit.

The flow rate, in litres per second, is easily calculated by dividing the total heating load in watts by 41 870 as explained in Chapter 6.

To calculate the circuit head loss, the index circuit must be determined. The index circuit is that route which has most friction; this occurs with long runs and/or high loads and can usually be judged by sight. In our example the route on the isometric includes sections A-B-C-D-E-F.

The load on each length of pipe along this route must be looked up in Table 6.2 (Chapter 6) where the head loss in milimetres per metre run for the size of pipe can be found. For example, section C carries 4839 watts. From Table 6.2 this produces a head loss of 58 mm per metre. This section has a double run 7 m long, making 14 m of 15 mm pipe. The head loss is therefore 812 mm (14 × 58 mm).

When the head losses of all sections of the index circuit have been worked out in this way, they are totalled and either 30 or 35 per cent is added to allow for fittings as mentioned in Chapter 6. The result is the head loss that the pump has to overcome.

Note that in a fully pumped system, the cylinder load may be on the index circuit and would have to be allowed for just like another radiator.

Feed and expansion cistern

The feed and expansion cistern is situated as high as possible and is connected according to the type of system. In this example it is connected to the primary circuit. In fully pumped and two-tapping boiler circuits, it would be connected differently as explained in Chapter 8.

Controls

It is helpful to mark on the isometric any pipework controls such as diverter valves, zone valves etc. If you do not, it is quite possible to follow your layout enthusiastically and fix a beautiful run of pipework only to find you should have fitted a valve some feet back.

We now have the heat losses, the radiator sizes, the pipe runs and the pump selected. All that is needed is the boiler size.

13

Boiler sizing and fuel costs

In most books on central heating very little space is devoted to sizing the boiler. Generally when all the heat losses are totalled, a percentage margin is added plus any requirement for hot water, and that is the boiler output. Of course it works, but with a bit more thought it may be possible to employ a boiler with a smaller output and so save expense.

One of the aspects least understood by the trade itself, let alone the DIY installer, is the relationship between boiler size, system size, capital cost and running costs.

Air-change losses

At first sight it appears that the heating load that the boiler must provide for is the total of all the rooms, but this is not quite correct.

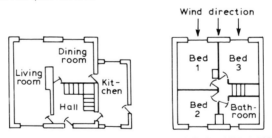

ROOM	FABRIC LOSS(W)	AIR CHANGE LOSSES (W)		
		DESIGN LOSS	FACTOR	ALLOWED TOTAL
Living room	2318	836	1·00	836
Dining room	1027	418	0·75	314
Kitchen	1771	542	1·00	542
Hall	134	323	0·50	162
Landing	−102	81	—	—
Bedroom 1	784	135	0·50	68
Bedroom 2	651	105	0·50	53
Bedroom 3	778	120	0·50	60
Bathroom	1036	437	0·50	219
Totals	8397	2997		2254

Total fabric + design air changes (8397 + 2997) = 11,394 W
Total fabric + allowed air changes (8397 + 2254 = 10,651 W

Fig. 13.1. Except in structures with no internal partitions, the boiler never supplies heat for the total of individual room air-changes. In the sample house, a reduction of 743W can be made from the total, as shown above

The individual rooms' heating requirements for the house shown in plan form total 11 394 watts. However, not all the air-change losses need be allowed for. For example, if the wind is acting in the direction of the arrows in Fig. 13.1, the cold air will infiltrate bedrooms 1 and 3 and push already-warmed air from these rooms into the bathroom and bedroom 2. The warm air in these rooms will be pushed outside but, although they have lost warm air, the radiators in bedroom 2 and the bathroom will not have to heat any cold air and so long as the wind stays in the same direction, they will never need to.

With the wind in the opposite direction, cold air will enter bedroom 2 and the bathroom and the radiators in those rooms will have to heat this air. As we cannot tell at the design stage in which direction the wind will blow, we must allow for all possibilities and size each radiator to allow for its having to warm cold air. But at any one time only two out of the four rooms are heating the cold air; therefore the boiler need provide only 50 per cent of the total upstairs air-change loss.

If there were no partition walls upstairs then the full air-change loss would need to be allowed for. The percentages to allow for different internal layouts are given in Table 13.1.

Table 13.1 Percentage of individual air-changes allowed in boiler sizing

Openings in room	Fraction of air-change loss to be counted towards total load
On three sides	1.00
On two opposite sides	1.00
On two adjacent sides	0.66
On one side but open plan to room with window opening on opposite side	0.75
On one side only	0.50
No openings	0.00

If we apply the percentages from Table 13.1. to our sample house we arrive at the 'allowed' air-change losses. As you can see, the total required is reduced from 11 394 watts to 10 651 watts. This may not seem much and on its own it is not important but there are so many areas where oversizing can take place (even though each may be small) that the total can cause 20 to 30 per cent oversizing.

Boiler margin

The total 'allowed' heat loss of 10 651 watts would be the boiler output needed, without hot water of course, if the building were to be heated continuously. However, most domestic systems are operated intermittently and this has an effect on the boiler size.

As explained in Chapter 2, the power required for warm-up is greater than that needed for the steady heat transmittance requirement so, at the outside design temperature, a system designed just to cope with the heat losses would not have enough power to warm up a building which had cooled from its designed operating temperature.

Of course, when the outside temperature is higher than the design temperature, the heating requirement will be less and there will be spare power for warming up the structure. To run intermittently at the design temperature, however, the system and the boiler must be capable of providing more than the heat losses alone.

No matter how much larger we make the boiler to provide the warm-up boost, it cannot warm up the structure instantaneously. Obviously the greater the margin of power over the normal design requirements, the shorter will be the pre-heat period but where do you draw the line with regard to size? Apart from the cost of a large boiler there is the question of efficiency.

Boiler efficiency

Each central heating boiler has an efficiency rating which is the percentage of the energy contained in the fuel which it can convert to useful energy. The rating is sometimes given for different operating loads but it is more usual for the rating to be for the boiler under maximum load. Efficiency reduces with reducing loads but the relationship is not in a straight line. A typical efficiency curve might show an efficiency at full load of 80 per cent but at half load the efficiency does not reduce to 50 per cent but might be 76 per cent. Even at only 5 per cent load the efficiency could still be 54 per cent.

Most days present a smaller load than the boiler is capable of, and so its seasonal efficiency must be less than maximum efficiency. The larger the boiler, the shorter the warm-up period, but also the worse the efficiency over the season.

Seasonal efficiency of central heating boilers is often argued about. Manufacturers claim high levels and electricity boards have been known to make ridiculously low estimates of seasonal efficiency in order to press the claims of electricity to be competitive. One way of checking seasonal efficiency is to run a boiler throughout a season and measure the fuel used in relation to the heat provided for the various outside temperatures. But this tells us only about one boiler for one season, which might have been very mild or very severe.

Another way to predict seasonal efficiency is to use the efficiency graph with tables showing the number of days at each temperature level in an average year. This is impossibly tedious without a computer but with one it gives a useful guide. This brings us to the idea of degree days.

Degree days

To get some idea of running costs, we need to have some idea of the average year's heating requirement and to help in this the Standard Degree-day was devised. This is based on an outside temperature of 15.5°C; the difference between this base and the actual outside daily mean temperature, multiplied by the number of days on which it occurs, gives the number of degree-days.

For example, if the mean outside temperature on a particular day were 4°C lower than the base at 11.5°C, this would be counted as four degree-days. If this temperature continued for 15 days then 60 degree-days would have occurred (4 × 15).

The accumulated degree-days for the whole year is a measure of the work the heating system will have to perform, and is therefore proportional to running costs.

The standard degree-day assumes that no heat is needed to produce a temperature of 18.3°C inside when the outside is at the base of 15.5°C (the reason for the odd temperatures is that they are straight conversions from the original 60°F and 65°F). One shortcoming of this method for present-day use is that it was developed when almost all central heating was in public buildings such as hospitals, schools and offices; and when 65°F was considered a luxurious temperature.

It also makes an arbitrary allowance for casual heat gains inside and from the sun outside, to give around 3°C difference without any heating. This is the effect averaged over the year but on a particular day there may be no casual heat gains. This makes it difficult to relate size of system, which is proportional to full design temperature difference, to seasonal running costs, which allow for an average 3°C less.

I have therefore prepared a completely different set of degree-day tables, which are more useful for modern domestic heating. They are based on 30-year averages of sunshine and temperature from more than 100 meterological stations. Instead of a seasons figure to a fixed base temperature, Table 13.2 shows the number of days at each mean daily temperature level and allows for solar radiation in an average year for the different latitude bands on the map in Fig. 13.2. This new system allows you to ascertain the degree days for your system at whatever inside temperatures you have chosen.

Table 13.2 Number of days in year at mean daily temperatures

°C	Mean daily temperature between and	°C	50°N to 51°N	51°N to 52°N	52°N to 53°N	53°N to 54°N	Latitude bands 54°N to 55°N	55°N to 56°N	56°N to 57°N	57°N to 58°N	58°N to 59°N
24	and	25	16								
23	and	24	27	18							
22	and	23	22	28	18						
21	and	22	19	24	28	20					
20	and	21	17	20	25	29	20				
19	and	20	16	17	21	26	30	21			
18	and	19	15	16	18	22	26	30	23		
17	and	18	15	15	17	18	22	26	31	23	
16	and	17	15	15	16	16	20	23	27	32	25
15	and	16	15	15	15	16	17	21	24	28	35
14	and	15	15	15	15	16	17	18	20	25	30
13	and	14	15	15	15	16	17	18	19	21	26
12	and	13	15	15	15	16	17	18	19	21	23
11	and	12	14	15	15	16	17	18	19	20	22
10	and	11	14	14	15	16	17	18	19	20	21
9	and	10	14	14	15	16	17	18	19	20	21
8	and	9	14	14	15	16	17	18	19	20	21
7	and	8	14	14	15	15	17	17	19	20	21
6	and	7	14	14	15	15	16	17	18	20	21
5	and	6	13	14	15	15	15	17	18	20	20
4	and	5	12	13	14	15	15	16	17	18	19
3	and	4	10	12	12	12	12	12	13	13	14
2	and	3	8	9	10	10	10	10	10	11	11
1	and	2	6	7	7	8	8	8	8	8	8
0	and	1	4	4	5	5	6	6	6	6	6
−1	and	0	3	3	3	4	4	5	5	5	5
−2	and	−1	2	2	3	3	3	4	4	4	4
−3	and	−2	1	2	2	2	2	3	3	3	4
−4	and	−3		1	1	1	2	2	2	3	3
−5	and	−4				1	1	1	2	2	2
−6	and	−5							1	1	2
−7	and	−6								1	1

Obviously you do not find a definite figure one side of a line and a different one on the other side; nor do all positions in the same band have exactly the same climate. However, considerations of space make it impossible to give all the variations, and the increase in accuracy would be marginal.

Table 13.2 can be used for running-cost calculations, as could the old method, (and I will be covering this later), but unlike the standard system it can be used to relate running costs to system size and to find boiler efficiency.

Seasonal boiler efficiency

I used a computer to work out the efficiencies of different types of boilers at varying load levels and different temperatures for the number of days involved. I did this for all stations and all temperature combinations from 18°C to 25°C inside and 0°C to −6°C outside and proved (unsurprisingly from a mathematical point of view) that the seasonal efficiencies did not reduce

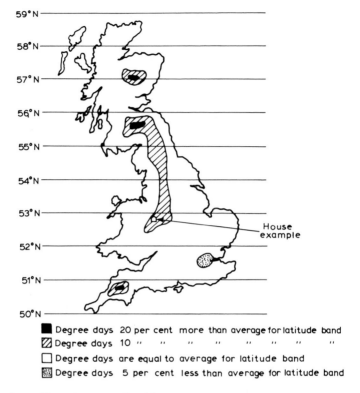

59°N

58°N

57°N

56°N

55°N

54°N

53°N

52°N

51°N

50°N

House
example

■ Degree days 20 per cent more than average for latitude band
▨ Degree days 10 ″   ″   ″   ″   ″   ″   ″   ″
□ Degree days are equal to average for latitude band
▦ Degree days 5 per cent less than average for latitude band

Fig. 13.2. Map to be used in conjunction with Table 13.2 to ascertain number of days at different temperatures and thus the degree-days

Table 13.3 Energy-producing efficiency

	Maximum efficiency (%)	Seasonal adjustment	
		HE system	LE system
Central heating			
Hand-stroked solid fuel	65 to 70	0.80	0.75
Automatic solid fuel	70 to 75	0.85	0.78
Gas fired	75 to 80	0.89	0.82
Oil fired	75 to 80	0.90	0.83
Unit heating			
Open fire	25 to 35	—	—
Gas fire	60 to 65	—	—
Paraffin heater	85 to 90	—	—
Bottled gas heater	85 to 95	—	—
Electric fire	100	—	—

The seasonal adjustment depends on whether the system is high efficiency (HE) or low (LE). A high-efficiency system would have a new boiler with low-water content and full controls, insulated where necessary. Because radiator panels placed correctly give a better comfort level at a lower air temperature than convected heat, a radiator system will also increase efficiency. A low-efficiency system would have an old boiler with just boiler thermostat control and no insulation. Most systems will be between the two extremes.

to anywhere near the levels some electricity board state, and they deviate no more than 1 per cent from the mean throughout all the variations.

The results are shown in simplified form in Table 13.3. The seasonal efficiency can be obtained by applying the seasonal factor to the boiler's stated maximum efficiency. An oil boiler of, say, 77 per cent will have a seasonal efficiency of 69 per cent (77 per cent × 0.90).

Very intermittent systems in heavy buildings, such as churches used once a week, need a system larger than the design heat loss by the building class number. A class 4 structure would ideally need a system providing four times the heat loss in order to match the rate at which the structure itself would absorb the heat.

In normally-operated domestic systems the temperature is unlikely to fall sufficiently to need a system more than 50 per cent larger than the design requirements in order to achieve a very rapid warm-up at the outside design temperature. But remember, the entire system would need to be 50 per cent larger and that much more expensive; its efficiency would fall and running costs rise.

Increased emission

Emission from radiators etc. depends on the difference in temperature between them and their surroundings. The lower the room temperature the greater the emission.

In normal domestic situations the inside temperature does not fall sufficiently for radiators to increase their emission by more than 20 per cent but we obtain this 20 per cent increase without increasing the size of the radiators. The only part we must increase in size is the boiler. There is obviously no point in increasing the boiler size by more than 20 per cent because the radiators can't emit more. If you want a bigger warm-up boost than this, you must increase the size of the whole system.

This fortuitous increase in emission is obviously a good reason for adding a margin to the heat loss in order to obtain the boiler size. It is a margin for intermittent operation and not, as I read so often, a margin for extra-low temperatures. If the radiators are sized for the heat loss then, regardless of how much larger the boiler is, they cannot emit more heat when the rooms are at the inside design temperatures, no matter how cold it is outside. They can emit more only when the room temperature is lower than the design temperature caused by the system being off for a period.

The fact that many people in the trade and writers continue to refer to this margin as a reserve for very cold weather shows lack of understanding. If you want a system to cope with extra-cold weather then it should be designed for a lower outside temperature.

Lower outside temperatures

With some recent very cold winters in mind, suppose you do want your system to cope with a lower outside temperature than the standard design temperature. If the average inside temperature is, say, 20°C and instead of −1°C outside, you want to design to −4°C, then the system will be larger. You will get your inside temperatures at the lower outside temperature but is it worth it?

If your house is between latitude 51°N and 52°N, you can see from Table 13.2 that, in an average year, there are two days when the temperature falls to −2°C, two other days when it falls to −3°C and one day only when it falls to −4°C. On that day, with a system based on the standard design temperature of −1°C, the temperature will reach 17°C instead of the 20°C required. When you think that the average person can easily cope with a 3°C drop by putting on a wool sweater, it hardly seems worth the expense of increasing the size of the system by around 14 per cent, which is what that lower design temperature would mean.

In the far north of Scotland, between latitude 58°N and 59°N, there are 16 days on average when the mean daily temperature is below −1°C and the maximum to make up by other means is an extra 6°C, which is more than an extra sweater could cope with. Here there may be a case for designing to a lower temperature. On the other hand it may be more cost-effective to switch on a small unit heater for just those few days in the year.

It is up to the individual to decide the trade-off between capital costs of equipment and the extra warmth it will give when needed on only a few days of the year. However, you can now work out your own figures, using Table 21, to help make the decision.

In the north of Scotland the degree-day total for average inside temperature of 19°C is 3590: on the south coast of England it is 2268 degree-days. The running costs are likely to be up to 60 per cent higher for the same house and the same inside temperatures. This point was made in the House of Commons after the very bad winter of 1983–1984 in Scotland and the North of England. A suggestion was made for some sort of energy allowance to be made but it seems a long way off.

Running costs

I have worked out a relatively simple method of estimating running costs for all systems. This method can be used regardless of price changes, because it allows you to use the prevailing price of whatever fuel you are considering when you actually do the calculation.

Annual energy need

The house we have been considering is a class 2 building. You can work out the energy needed for individual rooms or the whole house. For the whole house you need to know the average inside temperature and this is easily found by taking the volume of each room, multiplying this by its temperature and totalling the results. The total is then divided by the sum of the volumes and, in our sample house, the average comes to 19°C.

To demonstrate the method, suppose the house is located in the West Midlands as shown on the map, between latitude 52°N and 53°N. From Table 13.2 we can see that there are 18 days when the outside temperature is between 18°C and 19°C. On those 18 days the heating system is called upon to make up the 1°C difference, which is counted as 18 degree-days.

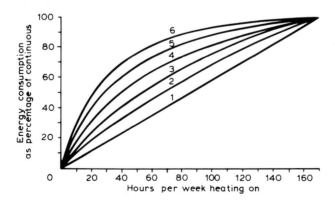

Fig. 13.3. Chart shows percentage of continuous energy used for various running times. The numbers against the curves are the class of building from Table 2.1 in Chapter 2

There are 17 days needing a 2°C lift from the heating system, which is equivalent to another 34 degree-days. Working down the 52°N to 53°N column in this way, we eventually come to three days between 0°C and −1°C when the full design temperature difference of 20°C must be made up; this adds a final 60 degree-days.

The accumulated figure will be 2438 degree-days. The house is in a shaded area, indicating a 10 per cent increase, which brings the total to 2682 degree-days. This represents an energy requirement over the season at varying loads related to the changing temperature differences from day to day.

If, for argument's sake, instead of running at different levels throughout the year, the degree-day total of 2682 days occurred in one period when the outside temperature was permanently at −1°C and we ran the system day and night at full load, the boiler would have to make up the 20 degrees every day. Each day would produce 20 degree-days so to cover 2682 degree days flat out, the system would run for 134.1 days or 3218 hours.

However, our system does not run continuously.

Effect of intermittent running

If the system runs for 12 hours a day, which is 84 hours per week, its energy consumption will not be half of the energy needed for continuous 24 hours a day operation, because of the extra needed to warm up the structure each time it is switched on. The percentage of continuous fuel consumption that will be needed is found from the energy consumption chart in Fig. 13.3.

The house is a Class 2 building, so we look up from the 84 hours per week operation to the Class 2 curve and then across to the left vertical scale, where 60 per cent is given. This means that to provide the energy for our 50 per cent actual operating time we use 60 per cent of the fuel used for continuous running. We know that if the system is operated full-time to provide the total seasonal requirement it must run for 3218 hours, but from a fuel consumption point of view it runs for 60 per cent of this, which is 1931 hours.

Efficiency adjustment

The power needed at the design temperatures is 10 651 watts or 10.651 kilowatts. If the energy used throughout the year is equivalent to this power applied for 1931 hours, then 20 567 kilowatt-hours will be needed (10.651kW × 1931 hours).

If the boiler were 100 per cent efficient, we would have to buy fuel containing 20 567 kWh of energy. But boilers and systems are not this efficient. If a modern radiator system with full controls employs a gas boiler with 80 per cent maximum efficiency, from Table 13.1, a factor of 0.89 might apply. The seasonal efficiency is therefore 71 per cent (80 per cent × 0.89). This means that we must buy fuel containing 28 968 kWh (20 567kWh/0.71) because only 71 per cent of this will be useful. Now we know how much energy must be bought we can work out the cost.

Fuel costs

Every fuel has a calorific value, which indicates its energy content, according to the unit of measurement. To confuse us, the fuels are sold in different units of volume or weight and, in the case of gas, by an imperial unit of energy. As we are working in the metric system and measuring everything in kilowatt-hours, I have used the calorific values of the various fuels to give a factor to apply to the units in which they are sold. To find the cost per kilowatt-hour of energy purchased, all you have to do is multiply the cost of the unit in pence by the factor. Thus for gas the factor, from Table 13.4, is 0.0341 and applies to the 'therm' which is what the gas boards charge for; if the cost per therm is, say, 35 pence, the cost per kilowatt-hour is 1.19p (35p × 0.0341).

Table 13.4 Energy costs

	Unit sold	Calorific factor
Central heating fuels		
Natural gas	therm	0.0341
Oil (28 sec)	litre	0.0982
Oil (35 sec)	litre	0.0947
Coal	50 kg	0.0024
Sunbright	50 kg	0.0026
Housewarm singles	50 kg	0.0024
Anthracite nuts	50 kg	0.0021
Anthracite grains	50 kg	0.0022
Bottled gas (LPG)	litre	0.1462
Bottled gas (LPG)	kg	0.0731
Unit heating fuels		
Bottled gas	kg	0.0731
Paraffin	gallon	0.0216
Electricity	kWh	1.0000

Multiply cost in pence per unit by calorific factor to give cost in pence of each kWh of energy bought.

For our example we need fuel containing 28 968 kWh so the cost of Gas will be £344.72 (28 968 kWh at 1.19p). If there is a standing charge this must be added.

A useful formula method of working out running costs follows, which can be used for any fuel at any price.

$$\text{Annual energy for heating} = \frac{DD \times 24 \times HL \times IE}{\Delta t \times 100} \text{kWh}$$

	Data	*Obtained from*
	DD = Degree-days	Fig. 13.2 and Table 13.2
	HL = Design heating load in kW	Heat-loss calculations
	IE = Intermittent energy %	Consumption chart and Table 2.1 (Chapter 2)
	Δt = Design temperature difference	Chosen temperature

For our sample system:

$$\frac{2682 \times 24 \times 10.651 \times 60}{20 \times 100} = \textbf{20 567 kWh.}$$

$$\text{Annual energy for hot water} = \frac{HW \times 65 \times 365}{1000} + ACL \text{ kWh}$$

	Data	*Obtained from*
	HW = Daily consumption in litres	Observation
		(average 75 to 130 litres per person per day)
	ACL = Annual circuit loss	Properly insulated about – 350 kWh/year

For our sample system, say three persons at 100 litres/day:

$$\frac{300 \times 65 \times 365}{1000} + 350 = \textbf{7467 kWh.}$$

Environmental temperature

It is not necessary to follow this section in order to design a domestic central heating system, since we have already done that in Chapter 12. However, some students may have come across environmental temperature and others may be interested in knowing about the concept.

In the beginning of this book I stressed the provision of comfort as being the whole purpose of central heating. We should therefore plan to produce an acceptable comfort temperature, not a particular air temperature. The traditional method of calculating heat losses, used room air temperatures to calculate all losses. But actually only the air-change losses are determined by the air temperature.

We have already covered the fact that the human body is affected by air and mean radiant temperature (MRT) on a 50/50 basis. However, the heat lost through a structure is influenced more by the MRT. The actual loss is found to be proportional to a temperature equal to two-thirds MRT and one-third air temperature. This is the environmental temperature and was originally envisaged by the CIBS and the Institute of Domestic Heating Engineers as a suitable measure of comfort as well as heat transfer, but it is now superseded by the proper comfort temperature (officially the dry resultant temperature).

However, from a strict calculation point of view, the fabric heat losses should be based on environmental temperature and the air-change losses on air temperature. It would be much easier to work to one temperature as I have done with the calculations in Chapter 12 and, since it is comfort we want, why not use the comfort temperature throughout? For those who are concerned that this may cause inaccuracy, I will compare results from using these two temperatures or just the comfort temperature.

As an example we can look at the losses of the living room in our sample house. The first thing is to establish the various temperatures in the room. The average U-value of the wall surfaces, including windows, is 1.85 W/m^2 °C. If we look at Table 1.2 in Chapter 1 we can see that for this average value and with three outside walls and a radiator system, the comfort temperature is 93 per cent of the air temperature. The comfort temperature I have used is 21°C, therefore the air temperature will be 21/0.93 which is 22.6°C. The comfort temperature is made up of half MRT and half air temperature. Half the air temperature of 22.6°C is 11.3°C, so if we take this from the comfort level of 21°C we obtain 9.7°C which must be half the MRT. The MRT must therefore be 19.4°C. The environmental temperature will be 20.4°C, i.e. one-third of 22.6°C (air temperature) plus two-thirds of 19.4°C (MRT).

In the sample house the living-room losses were calculated on a temperature difference of 22°C (21°C inside and −1°C outside) and were as follows:

Internal	203 watts
External fabric	2125 watts
Air change	836 watts
Total	3154 watts

Using the environmental temperature of 20.4°C for the fabric losses means that they will be calculated on a temperature difference of 21.4°C (with the outside at −1°C). The air-change losses will be calculated using a temperature difference of 23.6°C. The new figures are as follows:

Internal	203 watts
External fabric	2067 watts
Air change	896 watts
Total	3166 watts

The fabric losses are lower using this method and the air-change losses are greater. The end result differs by only 12 watts, which is about 0.3 per cent of the total. The human body can't detect that small a difference in loss and the best room thermostats have an accuracy of plus or minus 5 per cent.

You can see that as it is comfort we are aiming for, we should use the comfort temperature as our basis. To do otherwise is to make unnecessary work.

14
Installation

When you come to the practical side of your installation you exchange your white collar and calculator for overalls and a tool bag. This is the work that many people worry about. They may get specialist companies such as my own to design the system if they do not feel like doing that themselves, but if it is to be a do-it-yourself system this part can't be carried out by anyone else.

The practical skills required for a domestic heating system are not as difficult as for many plumbing jobs. Apart from the general work of drilling holes, lifting floorboards etc., there is only one area of manipulative skill directly related to the heating system: connecting the components using tube and fittings.

Tube

Because of its easier handling, copper is generally preferred to stainless steel except on the one or two occasions when the copper price has been much higher. The rigid copper tube used for domestic systems can be bent in 15 mm and 22 mm sizes only.

Microbore tube can be bent using external springs or tube benders, although the latter are expensive for only one installation.

Bending tube

To bend tube, the correct-size spring is inserted until its mid-point is where the bend is to be; the tube is then bent over the knee or around a wood former. If the tube is slightly overbent and pushed back a little, the spring will be easier to remove. A length of stiff wire should be attached to the eye of the spring if the bend is to be made some way down a length of tube; it is used to push the spring to its position and to remove it.

Cutting tube

A pipe cutter is preferable to a hacksaw because it produces a square cut and does not create as much swarf which, as you will recall from Chapter 9, is the cause of much corrosion. After it is cut the end is reamed.

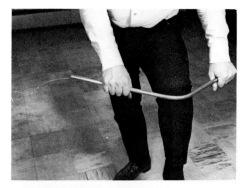
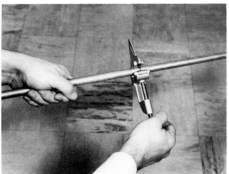

Fig. 14.1. Top left: tube being bent using a spring with wire attached. String is not a good substitute because it may break and the spring may be left inside and because it cannot be used to push the spring into position. Above: a pipe cutter is being used, and (left) the end of the cutter is used to ream out the end. The tube should be held so that any swarf falls out of and not into the tube

Fittings

There are four types of fittings and the procedure in each case is as follows:

Compression fittings

These fittings are made to produce a watertight joint without any sealing compound but I prefer to use some to be sure and to reduce the amount of tightening needed. These fittings have three

Fig. 14.2. Left: a Conex compression tee assembled prior to tightening. The right-hand olive is shown smeared with sealing compound. Right: fitting tightened

components: the body, the olive and the nut. The nut and olive are put onto the tube which is pushed up to the shoulder stop in the body of the fitting, a small amount of sealing compound is smeared onto the olive and the whole assembly is tightened. Some makes of fitting have an olive with steep taper on one side and a shallow taper on the other; in this case the shallow taper goes into the body of the fitting.

Solder-ring capillary fittings

The inside of the fitting is cleaned with steel wool and the appropriate flux applied. The end of the tube is then cleaned and this is smeared with flux. Fluxes are corrosive and fingers should not be used. The tube end is inserted into the fitting and rotated to distribute the flux evenly.

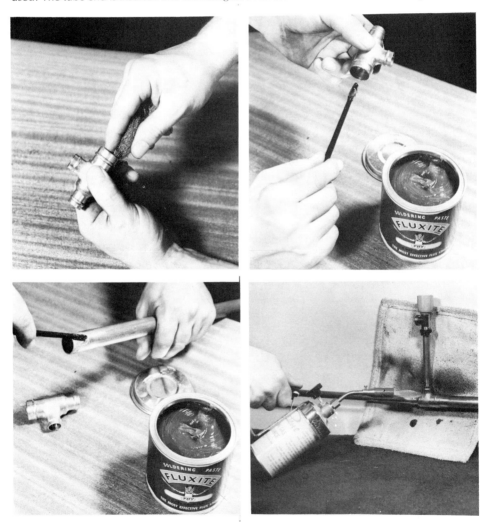

Fig. 14.3. Procedure for capillary fittings. Top left: cleaning inside fitting with steel wool. Top right: applying flux to fitting. Below left: applying flux to tube. The fitting should be cleaned and fluxed before the tube as it is easier to put down the fitting without disturbing the flux while the tube is being dealt with. Below right: heating the fitting using heat-resistant mat to protect surroundings. With end-feed fittings, a strip of solder must be held at each end in turn

Use a blowlamp to apply heat until a ring of solder appears at the mouth of the fitting, at which point it is left to cool. If the ring is incomplete, reheat to remove and replace the fitting or apply a strip of solder to the mouth of the fitting and reheat. Do not use too much flux. Although that remaining outside can be wiped off, any left on the inside can cause corrosion and, as it is not easily soluble in water, blockage of pumps, valves etc.

With these fittings it is difficult to heat one end alone without melting the solder at other ends. It is better therefore to make up all ends and apply heat at the same time. If this is not possible, wrap a wet cloth around the end or ends to be made up later.

End-feed capillary fittings

Proceed as for solder-ring fittings and when fitting is hot apply a strip of solder. Be careful to use the correct type of solder for the job. You should not use the electrician's solder containing flux.

If the blowlamp is used near the building fabric a fire-resistant mat should be used. The old mats were made of asbestos but the latest are of woven glass fibre.

Threaded fittings

Threads appear on many fittings which connect to components such as pumps, radiators etc. To make these watertight you can use strands of hemp wound into the threads, and then smearing sealing compound over the hemp. Alternatively you can use PTFE tape. Generally the tape is better on small fittings but reducing fittings used with large boiler tappings may need the hemp method.

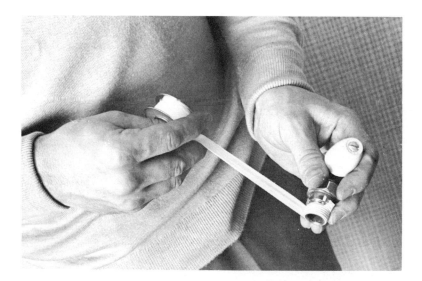

Fig. 14.4. PTFE tape being used to seal thread on radiator valve

Making a start

The best point to start the installation is with the emitters; whether they are radiators or other types, the first thing is to position these where you want, bearing in mind comfort conditions (see Chapter 1).

Radiators

Each radiator must be positioned so that there is at least 100 mm below it for fitting the pipework. The brackets for the radiators are fixed so that there is a very small rise to the air-vent end.

The most common method of fixing is by screwing into wall plugs; no. 10 gauge screws in $1\frac{1}{2}$ in to 2 in lengths are sufficient. If you have studded walls then a suitable cavity fixing must be used.

After the radiator is hung, the hand-control valve is fitted on the flow pipe; if thermostatic valves are used, the sensor can be left off at this stage. A lockshield valve is fitted on the return tapping.

Fan convectors

Fan convectors are fixed to the wall using the template supplied to locate the screw fixings. Usually there are either two copper pipe extensions or two compression fittings. In both cases in-line control valves can be fitted to perform the functions of radiator valves. However, as the unit has its own thermostatic control it is only necessary to fit a lockshield valve for balancing.

Skirting heating

Skirting heating can be fitted above the skirting board if it is the modern low type, but otherwise the skirting should be removed. In either case the makers' figures for minimum clearance above the floor must be followed.

Fig. 14.5. Section through Finrad skirting heating showing fins and damper control

Pipe runs

The pipework is best fitted running from each radiator back to where it joins other radiator circuits, following the design layout and using the correct-size tube.

It is best to use a power saw to cut across the floorboards and to cut between them to sever the tongue. The blade should cut only as deep as the boards: there may be electric cables below.

When a floorboard has been cut all round it can be lifted — sometimes it is possible to lever the board up and pull out the nails with it but often it is easier to punch the nails right through before lifting. In any case nails should be removed before replacing. The boards should not be nailed down until the system has been filled and the joints tested.

When pipework runs between joists, supports must be fitted at minimum intervals as shown in Table 14.1. When pipes cross joists they should be set into notches cut only as deep as is necessary to house the pipe and should be cut as close to the supported end of the joist as possible, as in Fig. 14.6.

Table 14.1 Intervals for pipe supports

Pipe diameter	Vertical	Horizontal
15 mm	2.0 m	1.5 m
22 mm	2.3 m	1.8 m
28 mm	2.6 m	2.2 m
35 mm	3.0 m	2.6 m

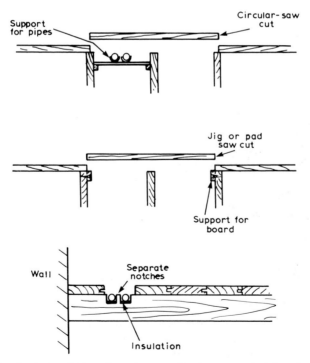

Fig. 14.6. With a circular saw the boards can be cut so that they rest on the joists when replaced but with other saws the cut must be made at the side of the joist, and some support must be made for the boards

Because of movement caused by expansion, clips should not be tightened directly on to the pipes as this will cause noise each time the system is heated or cools down. For the same reason long straight runs of pipe should not be held rigidly at each end.

When there is a solid floor downstairs, radiators may be supplied by dropping pipes from a main circuit in the upstairs floor. However, pipes can be placed in channels in the solid floor; these should not be set into concrete but should be insulated and covered with a removable board or metal cover.

When the tube passes through holes in the fabric of the building it must be separated from the structure by a suitable rot-proof insulating material. Ideally, when passing through walls, the pipe should ideally be sleeved with the next-sized tube as in Fig. 14.7.

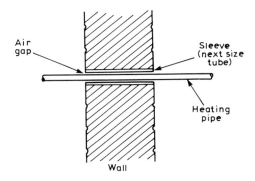

Fig. 14.7. The purpose of sleeving is to allow the heating pipes to expand without damaging plaster etc.

Cylinder

If the new indirect cylinder replaces an old direct one, the changeover should be made as quickly as possible to reduce the period without hot water. The procedure is as follows.

1.   If an immersion heater is fitted, isolate this by switching off and by removing the fuse. Then disconnect the wiring.

2.   Close the gate valve or stop tap if fitted in the supply pipe from the cold storage cistern to the base of the cylinder. If no valve is fitted, close the stop cock in the main supply to the ball valve or, using strong wire, tie up the ball valve to a length of wood placed across the top of the storage cistern.

3.   Open the hot taps until flow stops; the pipework will be empty and the cylinder full.

4.   If a drain tap is fitted to the feed near the base of the cylinder or at the boiler connect a hose to this and drain. If no drain is fitted, undo the top connection on the cylinder, having an absorbent cloth handy to deal with any seepage. Insert a hose and siphon to a lower level.

5.   When the cylinder is drained, remove the immersion heater.

6.   Replace the immersion heater into the new cylinder if required.

7.   Disconnect all pipework to the existing cylinder and remove it.

8.   Position the new cylinder and reconnect the pipework to the top connection and to the feed near the base. Some slight adjustment may have to be made if the position of the tappings are not exactly as they were for the previous cylinder. If no drain tap was originally fitted in the cold feed, fit one now to avoid having as much trouble in the future as you have just had emptying this one.

The cylinder can be refilled and used to supply hot water using the immersion heater. The two primary tappings which connect to the feed and return from the boiler can be left untouched for now. Air in the pipework to the taps will clear through the taps or the open vent to the storage cistern.

Feed and expansion cistern

The central heating system needs a feed and expansion cistern, which must be positioned according to the design and, if in a loft, should be put on a firm, rigid base placed across the joists.

Fig. 14.8. Feed and expansion cistern with ball valve and overflow positions visible

The feed and expansion pipe to the heating system is fitted about 25 mm from the base of the cistern. The open safety vent from the heating circuit rises above the cistern and is bent over so that it can discharge safely. An overflow pipe is fitted between 25 mm and 50 mm from the top of the cistern and should discharge to the outside; bearing in mind that the water may be very hot, it should also discharge in sight so that steps can be taken immediately to correct the condition.

The cistern is fed from the mains through a ball valve. This should be fitted higher than the overflow and the arm bent so that the valve shuts off when the cistern is about one-third full. If the valve is set so that the cold level is too high, expansion will cause overflowing every time the water is heated.

Obviously these adjustments can be made only after the system is filled. A stop cock should be fitted in the main feed pipe to the ball valve.

Boiler

Domestic boilers are divided into Class I (solid fuel and oil) and Class II (gas) appliances.

The internal layout and positioning of tappings in boilers vary so much, and the manufacturer's instructions which come in the boiler packing are so comprehensive, that there is no point in my trying to cover all the variations here. However, there are some points to emphasize.

All free-standing boilers must be positioned on a non-combustible surface. Depending on the weight of the boiler and the structural strength of a wood floor, and certainly in the case of Class 1 appliances, there may be a need to build a constructional hearth in concrete. Clearance dimensions around the appliance given in the instructions should be adhered to.

All boilers need a supply of air for combustion and if they do not get sufficient the fuel will not be burnt efficiently. The effects of this are higher costs, damage to the boiler and, most important, a possible build-up of poisonous gases.

With a room-sealed or balanced-flue gas boiler, the terminal fitted according to the manufacturer's instructions will automatically provide a balance between air in and flue gases out. With a conventional-flue boiler a permanent low-level inlet must be provided which cannot be closed.

A supply of air is also needed to ventilate the compartment in which the boiler is situated. This is necessary even if its combustion air is supplied through a balanced flue. Of course, if a boiler is placed in an open position in a kitchen it is likely to have sufficient ventilation from the usual door and window openings. But if fitted in a cupboard or similar, then open vents at high and low levels must be provided as in Table 14.2.

Table 14.2 Permanent vent areas per kW boiler rating

	Conventional flue		Room sealed	
Opening at	Air from room	Air from outside	Air from room	Air from outside
High level	9cm^2	4.5cm^2	9cm^2	4.5cm^2
Low level	18cm^2	9cm^2	9cm^2	4.5cm^2

Both low and high vent areas are required.

Flues

The regulations concerning flues and chimneys are now so complex that any attempt to cover them here in the space available could be misleading.

The regulations are different for Class 1 and Class 2 appliances. However, the basic rules are that only specially insulated flue pipes can pass through the house, they must not touch any combustible part of the house and they should rise to a height sufficient to avoid down-draughts and to discharge all the combustion gases.

They should be insulated on the outside, and for this purpose the modern twin-wall sectional flues illustrated in Fig. 14.9 are ideal. If an existing chimney is used, it should be suitably lined according to the type of boiler. Even the openings in a gas cowl are defined and must not exceed 15 mm to prevent birds entering. Deaths have occurred because this rule has been ignored.

If you are in any doubt, go to your local library and look up a copy of the Building Regulations and, if applicable, the gas safety regulations.

Fuel storage

There is no storage problem with gas, and solid-fuel storage is a matter of commonsense bearing in mind that central heating solid fuel is in small pieces and must be retained. With LPG gas, the supply company will provide and install the tank but with oil boilers you have to do it yourself.

The oil tank should be raised between 1 m and 1.5 m off the ground for the oil to reach the boiler by gravity; see Fig. 14.10. There must be good support as the tank and oil could weigh over 3 tons. A fire valve must be fitted to stop the oil supply if the boiler is overheated. If the tank is far from the road it may be necessary to provide an extension fill point for the tankers.

Fig. 14.9. Selkirk Metalbestos sectional twin-wall flues and chimneys are available for Class I and Class II appliances. There is a wide range of parts to fit any situation including a terminal housing which looks like a traditional chimney. Notice the square spacers which keep the flue the statutory distance from the structure

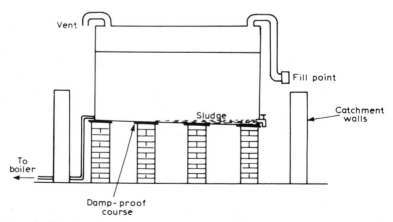

Fig. 14.10. An oil tank supported on brick piers on a minimum thickness of 150 mm concrete to take the considerable weight. The damp-proof course should be non-bituminous. The take-off end is raised about 30 mm higher to allow any residue to settle at the other. In case of leaks a catchment wall must be built to hold the volume of the tank plus 10 per cent

Controls and electrics

Many DIY installers still prefer to leave all the electrical connections to a qualified electrician. A great many professional installers do. However, it is possible to carry out all the wiring if the wiring instructions, which come with each piece of equipment, are followed exactly. The various combinations of controls make it impossible to go into detail, but the well-known manufacturers' diagrams are quite straightforward.

All current from the mains into the electrical control system must come through a fused spur, which may be switched for convenience. Care must be taken to ensure earth continuity throughout, primarily for safety of course. However, it is believed that the increase in the level of electrolysis in systems is due to the increasing use of electrical controls in which small stray currents occur.

When all wiring has been completed and all pipework is made up, including the connections to the primary side of the cylinder, and all the joints are checked, the system is ready for filling.

Filling up

The first step is to remove the pump and replace it with a length of pipe between the valves. The system should be flushed through a number of times without the pump to remove any swarf, which might jam the pump.

Open all valves and close all air vents; next, attach a hose to the lowest drain tap of the system leading outside, but keep the drain tap closed. Expose all joints and then start filling the system by opening the stop cock to the feed and expansion ball valve; the system will fill downstairs first and so the downstairs joints need to be checked for leaks before the upstairs.

Unless you have failed to check the joint at all so that it is quite loose, any leaks should be very small so don't panic. If a leak occurs on a compression joint, it probably just needs a bit more tightening.

However, a leaking capillary fitting needs to be remade after the system is emptied, since it is impossible to reheat a fitting with water inside it. To empty the system, close the stop cock to the cistern and open the drain tap.

Fig. 14.11. Masterflex pipe insulation from Barlo products being fitted on to pipe in the loft

If there are no leaks, pipes can be insulated and the cylinder jacket can be fitted unless you are using a foam-covered one. Starting with the downstairs radiators, open the air vents one at a time until water appears. When the whole system is filled, open the drain tap and allow water from the system to flush through for at least 15 minutes. Empty and flush through again.

When flushed through, close the pump valves and replace the tube with the pump. When the pump is running, the radiators will need venting again. At this point a corrosion inhibitor should be introduced into the system via the feed and expansion cistern. A wide range of inhibitors are made under the trade name Fernox and I have found this company's technical and advisory service excellent.

The actual commissioning of the boiler and the system can be carried out according to the manufacturer's instructions or, for a small fee, by gas boards, oil companies and boiler maintenance companies.

I recommend that you have this done for you, because the commissioning needs specialized equipment such as manometers and carbon-dioxide meters and is best left to experts. In any case, with a gas boiler you should use the gas board to make the supply connection of gas to the boiler. It is also sensible to arrange for a maintenance contract for the boiler.

Balancing

I have explained that the different sizes of tube have limits to the volume of water and hence the heating load that they can carry. If there were a size of tube for every radiator then exactly the right amount of water would get to each radiator and there would be no need for balancing.

However, one size of tube may be used to supply a number of different emitters but we want only the correct quantity of water to flow to each. The lockshield valve is used to accomplish this. Water normally takes the easiest path and with all valves open it will be found that some radiators are very hot and some may be quite cold. We must increase the resistance of the emitters which are getting hot and so send the water to the colder ones.

To begin with: open all valves completely. Thermostatic valve sensors are normally left off until after balancing.

The radiators which have little resistance between them and the pump will be hotter than others and the lockshield valves on these will need to be closed down more to restrict the flow. It is really a trial-and-error operation and you will find yourself going back and forth quite a bit before the distribution is correct.

In the initial stages a rough balancing can be carried out by touch on the radiator surface. We have planned for a 10°C temperature drop across each radiator so, if a pipe thermometer is put on the flow and another on the return, a more accurate balance should be possible. Unfortunately I have never found a pipe thermometer at a reasonable price to be any more accurate than using my sense of touch, looking at a room thermometer and using some judgment. The final balance is best carried out by monitoring the air temperature in each room when the outside temperature is at the design level.

When the system is balanced, the caps can be put on the lockshield valves and the sensors on any thermostatic valves. The hand-control valves can now be used for local adjustment without upsetting the basic balance set by the lockshield valves.

At this point an onlooker cannot tell the difference between a system which will last only two years and one which will last 20 years. But if you have taken note of the many points I have made dealing with hidden dangers of pumping over, overflowing, air entrapment, electrolysis, corrosion etc. and you have the boiler serviced regularly, yours will be the one to last and give you trouble-free comfort.

Useful addresses

General

British Gas Corporation, 326 High Holborn, London WC1V 7PT.
Chartered Institution of Building Services, 49 Cadogan Square, London SW1X 0JB. Tel: 01-235 7671.
Institute of Domestic Heating Engineers, 37a High Road, Benfleet, Essex. Tel: 037-45 54266.
Solid Fuel Advisory Service, Hobart House, Grosvenor Square, London SW1X 7AE. Tel: 01-235 2020.

Products

Boilers

Baxi Heating, P.O. Box 52, Bamber Bridge, Preston PR5 6SN. Tel: Preston 36201.
TI Glow-Worm Ltd., Nottingham Road, Belper, Derby DE5 1JT. Tel: 077-382 3741.
TI Parkray, Park Foundry, Belper, Derby DE5 1WE. Tel: 077-382 3741.
Potterton International Ltd., Portobello Works, Emscote Road, Warwick CV34 5QU. Tel: 0926 493420.
Rayburn, Glynwed Appliances Ltd., P.O. Box 30, Ketley, Telford, Shropshire TF1 1BR. Tel: 0952 51177.
Stelrad Group Ltd., P.O. Box 103, National Avenue, Hull, North Humberside HU5 4JN. Tel: 0482 492251.
Thorn-EMI Heating Ltd., Eastern Avenue, Team Valley Trading Estate, Gateshead, Tyne and Wear NE11 0PG. Tel: 0632 872211.
Trianco Redfyre Ltd., Stewart House, Brook Way, Kingston Road, Leatherhead, Surrey KT22 7LY. Tel: 0372 376453.
U.A. Engineering Ltd. (Bosky), Canal Street, Sheffield S4 7ZE. Tel: 0742 21167/738803.

Controls

Drayton Controls (Engineering) Ltd., West Drayton, Middlesex UB7 7SP. Tel: 08954 44012.
Honeywell Control Systems Ltd., Charles Square, Bracknell, Berkshire RG12 1EB. Tel: 0344 24555.
Randall Electronics Ltd., Ampthill Road, Bedford MK42 0ER. Tel: 0234 64621.
Satchwell Sunvic Ltd., Watling Street, Motherwell ML1 35A, Scotland. Tel: 0698 66277.
Smiths Industries Ltd., Environmental Controls, Waterloo Road, Cricklewood, London NW2 7OR. Tel: 01-379 7945.

Fittings

Conex Sanbra Ltd., Whitehall Road, Tipton, West Midlands. Tel: 021-557 2831.
Jeavons Engineering PLC, Lower Church Lane, Tipton, West Midlands DY4 7PH. Tel:
    021-557 3911.
Wednesbury Tube, Oxford Street, Bilston, West Midlands WV14 7DS. Tel: 0902 41133.

Flues

Selkirk Metalbestos, Household Manufacturing Ltd., 10 Lower Grosvenor Place, London
    SW1W 0EN. Tel: 01-828 7226.

Insulation

Disbotherm Ltd., 12 Mount Ephraim Road, Tunbridge Wells, Kent TN1 1EE. Tel: 0892 44822.
Fibreglass Ltd., St Helens, Lancs. Tel: 0744 24022.

Pumps

Grundfos Pumps Ltd., Leighton Buzzard, Bedfordshire. Tel: Leighton Buzzard 374876.

Radiators, skirting heating

Barlo Products Ltd., Barlo House, Foundry Lane, Horsham, West Sussex RH13 5TQ.
    Tel: 0403 62342.
Dia-Norm UK Ltd., Unit 290, Hartlebury Trading Estate, Nr. Kidderminster, Worcestershire.
    Tel: 0299 250108.
Finrad Ltd., 62 Norwood High Street, London SE27 9NP. Tel: 01-670 6987.
Myson Domestic Products Ltd., Ongar, Essex CM5 9RE. Tel: 0277 326222.
Stelrad Group Ltd., P.O. Box 103, National Avenue, Hull, North Humberside HU5 4JN.
    Tel: 0482 492251.
Thorn-EMI Heating Ltd., Eastern Avenue, Team Valley Trading Estate, Gateshead, Tyne and
    Wear, NE11 0PG. Tel: 0632 872211.

Towel rails

Midland Brass Fittings Co. Ltd., Wynford Road Industrial Estate, Birmingham B27 6JJ.

Acknowledgement

The author would like to thank the manufacturers listed above, who have provided details of their products for reproduction.

Index